The Answer Within

by
Bobby Banks

The Answer Within
by
Bobby Banks

Table of Contents

FOREWORD

In this rapidly changing world, people are looking for answers that will allow them to rebuild their lives. According to the U.S. Department of Labor, over 20,000 people are losing their jobs every single month. In fact, statistics indicate that in less than 10 years, 47 million people will be replaced by artificial intelligence. The question becomes: What do we do now?

Bobby Banks, gifted author, talented musician and speaker, has written a book called, "The Answer Within." The answer is within you on how to begin to rethink your life, how to begin to pick yourself up, and start all over again.

Willy Jolly said that, "A setback is a setup for a comeback." You have comeback power. You will find the answer…within you to begin to pursue a new path with your life.

Each chapter is written to expose you and take you to a place within yourself that you would never go by yourself. Each word is written so that you can begin to get an expanded vision of yourself beyond your adverse circumstances and mental conditioning; getting out of your head and stepping into your greatness.

Bobby, being the messenger, also has the message. He has overcome a great deal. He has experienced losing someone that he loves very much in his life. He has used his career as a musician to inspire, motivate, and move people with his music. Now he is writing to help you begin to navigate this new world we are in. The late Peter Drucker calls this time period, "The Era of the 3 C's: Accelerated Change, Overwhelming Complexity, and Tremendous Competition."

You have something special. You have greatness within you, and that greatness is the answer to how you will begin to live your life from a place of power. God asked Adam, "Adam, where are you?" Not because He didn't know, but because He wanted him to think. Because the answer to his dilemma was within him.

Life is a question and how you live your life is the answer. This book, this ground-breaking empowerment material, is designed to remind you that the answer is within you. "Seek ye first the Kingdom of God and all of His righteousness, and all things will be added unto you." When shall the Kingdom come? The Kingdom of God is within you.

Again, you have something special. You have greatness within you. This book will change your life. Read it and pass it on.

I'm Les Brown. . . Bobby, you've done yourself proud.

-Les Brown

PREFACE

So many times we read stories with themes meant to direct us toward making the best of everything until the best comes.

The best is already happening for you, and this is more than a story. This is not a book of motivational phrases or a compilation of self-help teachings. This is your life!

Oh. . . It's real, and you have no other choice than to digest the things you will read and allow the information to shape the new you. Allow The Answer Within to move you into your newness.

Do as I have done. . . Poco a poco, little by little—that is how we eat a cow. If you try to eat the entire cow in one sitting, you will moo yourself into the field and start eating grass. However, if you eat a few burgers one day, invite your family over for a few steaks the next, and do not forget to make yourself a few nice leather coats, not before too long the cow is gone, and you and your family are much better.

In closing, as within the paragraphs of this book and the beginning of your new life, read a little each day, live a little each day, and share a little with family and friends; share until the pages start to read *you*.

I know the pages in this book are for you, your surrounding family members, and your friends. The words only come through me—but to you, '*The Answer Within*' belongs.

Don't you dare stop. Your newest is within.

-Bobby

CHAPTER 1
LET'S GET A HOUSE

I'm going to tell you the story about how I went from living with rodents scurrying around outside of my apartment to having an in-ground pool in my own backyard—

After a major setback in my life, I was living in Brooklyn, New York wondering who I would turn to when all else seemed to fail. In spite of my hidden stress, I was traveling and enjoying the finer luxuries life had to offer. I would return home to the apartment I had only just moved into feeling discontent with my space and as though I should strive for more. I remembered that my very own mother had successfully been the owner of a multi-family home.

During this time of my life, the meager apartment I was living in didn't even have room for a dining table. My family and I had to sit and eat at a puny table with four tiny chairs around it. Being a man of opulence, I desired more for my dining area. A few months after moving in, I ordered a dining room set with eight chairs along with a full-sized breakfront from a furniture dealer in Israel. Was I going crazy?

When the furniture arrived several months later, the box was so big that it blocked the hallway and the entryway to my apartment. After the table was fully assembled, the quickest way to get to the back of the apartment was to actually crawl under the table. We joked that we had to go under the table and through the woods to Grandma's house. Boy, was it a journey!

I had lived in the area off and on for practically my entire life. When my mother and father first moved to the neighborhood the street was very quiet. As time went by, we began to acquire some unsavory neighbors as well as an accompanying host of creepy crawly comrades.

Inside the house we were very clean, and we thoroughly managed to keep the rodents at bay; however, outdoors was a much different story. Some evenings it was a nightmare to get inside of my residence due to the aforementioned furry pests not letting me into the building. I would have to flash my brights in their direction and they would quickly scurry from their haven right outside of my front door. I remember coming home to my apartment at 1 a.m. after producing a concert; I high beamed the rats and waited for my headlights to do their usual work. The creatures were not affected by my light show on this particular occasion and were not allowing me to go inside, so I had to drive onto the sidewalk in order to park closer to the entrance. Needless to say, I ran inside all the while screaming at the top of my lungs. I wound up disturbing both the neighbors and the rats that night. I had finally had enough and decided to buy my family a house on Long Island. I sat down at my oversized table, and with a pen and paper—I found the answer within.

In my mind I began to envision the front of a gorgeous house with a sprawling lawn. On the piece of paper I wrote down all of the amenities I wanted for my new residence. I went deep into my mind's eye and admired gorgeous fixtures in the living room and kitchen. I walked along dark hardwood floors, through the perfectly painted hallway, and into my cozy yet spacious bedroom. The next morning, I began to see my new home all around me. As I walked down the street, I saw ads for beautiful houses on the sides of buses all along Pitkin Avenue. At the store, all I could find were magazines about homes—I even went to the record shop and each section of music I perused added to my bewilderment; a few of the albums I had stopped to admire showed beautiful homes depicted in the details of the cover art! I knew that the intentions I had written were coming to pass. I couldn't wait!

A few Saturdays later, I went to have some fliers made for an upcoming concert at Friendship Baptist Church. I had been producing events at the popular church venue on Herkimer Street. When I arrived at the printing facility in West Hempstead, Long Island, I spotted a pamphlet of homes for sale. The houses in the brochure were of a much different style than what I had been envisioning, but I was intrigued! Surprisingly, the homes had driveways and attached garages. The streets were lined with perfectly manicured foliage, and there seemed to be plenty of street parking for guests. I could feel the tranquility of the neighborhood through the photos and I was in love.

While I was waiting for the printer, I noticed a realty office on the corner just a few doors down. With no money in my pocket I strutted in, and I inquired about the houses for sale. The woman at the desk was rather kind and gentle, and I could tell that she had a clear idea of my desires. After several minutes of talking, she drove me to a magnificent single family home. I almost fell out! This house was everything that I wanted and more. It was a single story ranch with a huge living room, central air, and a massive master bedroom. The home had a large front yard and an even bigger back yard with an above-ground pool. As soon as I saw it, I envisioned having an in-ground pool put in. The future-highlight reel of my cousins swimming and family members having a pool party, of course, started playing on repeat in my head. The house even had a dining room area large enough to fit my enormous dining set!

Two days after initially speaking with the proprietor, he called and asked me if I would like to take his place off the market and move forward with the purchase of his home. He told me we could work out the logistics on our own. Soon I met with the owner in person, and I told him how much I desired the house he had put up for sale.

I shared with him my heart: I explained that I was a teacher, how I was doing my best to save and keep up with bills, and that I was interested in the property. I also told him about how I wanted to bring my children to a place that was safe, with great schools.

What happened next was as assured as putting my right foot into my next step and walking forward. Ironically, and totally unbeknownst to me, the gentleman who owned my dream residence was also an educator! He recognized my path and understood my finances. We genuinely bonded with one another. Both of us knew what it was like to work our tails off and feel like we were never able to get too much further ahead in savings. I told him about my salary, and he became a mentor to me. After speaking to him over coffee, I would go outside and put my hands on the trees in his yard. I would walk around the property and visualize my life there. My salary at the time was minuscule at best, and since we both had teaching careers, him being much older than I was, he helped me make sense of my budget. He listened to me. My mentor never instructed me on how to proceed nor did he have to rationalize what needed to be done. I had the answers. He just listened.

The owner of the home was a great listener—he probed and I spoke. Through talking out loud to someone and communicating my ideas to a person who connected with me, I heard myself saying the truth of my reality. *Everything came from within.* As I look back now, I can say with certainty that I spoke myself into this successful journey. He never said, "Let me give you this." He allowed me to share the answer I had within myself. We worked out what I could afford to pay. With his help, I ascended and ultimately achieved my goal. October of 1991, I claimed it, and December 22nd, I moved in.

Before I had connected with the owner, I had begun realizing a lot about myself. I was unhappy with some of the social circles I was involved in. The antecedent to this shift in perspective involved self discipline and strong, advertent displays of self care in order to climb out of the hole I had not realized I had dug for myself. To be perfectly honest, I was knee deep into a lifestyle that took more from me than it ever gave. I didn't express any of these difficulties to the owner, as this was something I needed to check within myself. As I look back now, it is clear that I was reaching a new stage in my development. I was in the process of changing directions and leveling up my consciousness. More importantly, I was figuring out that the answers were inside of me. By now I had seen and witnessed where in my life I was capable and how I could go further. I followed my own breadcrumb trail and realized that my personal success stories had always materialized from thought. These pivotal confirmations were exactly what was needed to commence my new vision. This metamorphosis ushered in new confidence toward who I was and fortified a keen awareness of the control I had over the direction of my life. The key was in my thoughts and the voice I knew belonged to God when He was speaking to me.

I reflected about everything and anything that had been shown to add to the difficulty of hearing God's voice. I knew I had to change the type of people I was used to being around. It became a priority for me to carry myself in the ways that were most true to who I was. I needed to be 100% confident and exude my best personality in order for opportunities much more conducive to my needs to come my way. My dreams were real and tangible, but I had to find my center first. I knew I was placed on this earth to do more and to live a better life. The only way I could hear the answers to the questions I was asking was if I tuned in very acutely to the messages coming from within myself.

When you are finding your way again after developing the learned patterns and behaviors attributed to society's programming, you have to get to know yourself better in the light. One thing that many of us have in common is that we each possess insurmountable and palpable amounts of joy. The spirit of God lives within man even when man is living through what could decidedly be, upon looking back, some of our darkest days. We can often be unaware that people, without malice or ill-will, are attracted to the same spark and joy they're seeing radiating from others. It could also be that sometimes people in our social circles don't always know how to walk in their light while living out the demands of this world. As a result, we make friends with people that love our light because we always have it on. The love you make them feel ignites them. The point is, people will appreciate the good times and the fun they're having; they might even appreciate you and explicitly acknowledge you for what you offer them. While this appreciation is certainly love for what we know it as at the time, and the type strong enough to develop deep bonds, those of us who are conditioned to please others have to begin to learn what it means to be in the world and not of it. If you live to please the world, you will inevitably neglect your basic needs because you will tune into a different frequency for satisfying passing fads. Trust that at your core, you are your best self. Your suit of heavenly armor, tailored to fit only you, never goes out of fashion.

There is a destiny written for you. This destiny is the deepest bond ever forged, and it is your plan; the actuating sentiment of your internal navigating voice. And the good news is it's better than what a person even at their highest point can expect or even imagine. The answer within is the answer that only you can navigate, of course, with the selective help and assistance you will invariably be guided toward.

There's nothing wrong with serving others and being resourceful with wealth and knowledge; in fact, it's what we are here for. Consistently staying connected and being an instrument on this earth is our purpose and our calling. When it comes to friendship, envision first what kind of friend you want to be. We can agree to relationships with people who feed off of the moments when we make them feel alive and do not pour back into us. We are meant to cross paths and have relationships with these companions, because they assist us in our journey toward *knowing*. With their help we will grow to realize that, without a shadow of a doubt, *The Answer is Within*.

The truth is we need balance, because everything takes work and effort. The answer within tells me that I can assist others more when my very own house is abundant and when my cup is runneth over. Being aware of the wisdom inside of us means that we can access an endless flow of resources which can be utilized within our homes for our families; in our neighborhoods with our neighbors, in our schools for our kids, and be used to live well in a nation shared with people from every culture and ethnicity.

Oftentimes our neighbors, ourselves, and close associates can't understand the negative effects taking place in life, because we are yet to truthfully examine how to honestly care for ourselves. If we seek harmony but have inadvertently created an imbalance inside of us by making it a habit to neglect what the answer within tells us to do, even things as seemingly simple as keeping organized, clean, and focused will be difficult; resulting in every area of our lives being poorly impacted. These discrepancies will lead to not quite having enough of what we should be offering from abundance, and what we give will undoubtedly seem to come by way of suffering; making giving feel like an injustice. The answer within bolsters us and creates never endling supplies of energy that we need in order to win. If it's your mission in life to share and promote and assist, then you need to listen to your answer within as it blossoms like the apple tree of life. Listen when your thoughts are promoting positive ideas for you and assisting you.

Imagine a person surrounded by people. Everyone's carefree at first, and the people are all excited, because excitement is contagious. This example of mimicry can make folks think they've found their friend group and they start to make sacrifices to appease their new friends-turned-family. Do we live for a friend group or is there more to life? Somewhere along the line, if you're not sure of yourself and your answer within, you can get absorbed and entangled with others down a path that serves no one and least of all you. Many times what people do to make you feel good isn't always meeting the high bar of standards most suitable for your body, mind, and spirit.

We are all here making sense of life and the choices around us. What people tend to do for themselves or for you may not be the best. "Hey, hey, Bobby, you're the man!" It turns out, in the circle you are in, you're the one giving, paying, buying, loaning, providing the ride, and sharing the break you finally caught. You may think they're your friends, but they are actually only people who know you. They are people who make you believe their desire to be with you is attributed to their liking of you and how much they love you. It may be that their role in your life is shorter than you expected it to be. Look for the silver lining. You've acquired the catalyst you needed to put yourself on a path toward getting to know yourself better.

You must recognize how loved you are and what 'love' is. The only way you're going to know is by finding God's voice within yourself and recognizing Him as the answer. Reaching toward the potential you hold within is very becoming. How can you 'become' if you're caught up in damaging and demeaning cyclical habits?

Your internal alarm system might start to go off in regards to this existential wake up call sooner than those in your group. The question ends up being: will you rely on another's laissez-faire attitude toward what you feel about YOUR life? We all know what it feels like to bring a problem to a friend or family member only to feel like the person didn't quite get the conviction within our words. The truth is no one is going to look at the watch on your wrist for you. You have to be the one to decipher the hands on the coded face of your life and tell the time. You need to get your heart aligned with the truth of your existence and let the love flow inwards. You have to become you. It's time. This authentic love that is provided for you smoothes over and heals any nicks, scrapes, and wounds previously sustained. Your ability to listen to the voice inside speak to you and show you that there's more and better for you in this life will fortify you so that you can move through your journey, traversing obstacles and challenges, without further damaging yourself and others.

Eventually your answer within, which you steadily continue to recognize, can be an antenna to link up with others who get the picture. Now because you have leveled yourself up, it's clear the type of connections you feel your best toward making. How are you going to know how something feels unless you've felt it before? This includes the good and the bad. . . And even the ugly. During our adolescence kids can be cruel, the world can seem daunting, and we pick up on some poor habits within the realm of self worth. Not everyone around you has gotten to know who they are well enough yet to love themselves completely; we are all still on our missions. Your mission is about you. If you don't know how to love yourself or what that means, you're going to be attracting people who don't know either while normalizing and accepting the bare minimum. When you are inexperienced in the art of truly loving and accepting your journey, you inevitably end up gradually gaining the skills you need from a natural process. This measured process begins when you decide to commit to your growth.

The truth that continues to be reiterated to you through every experience you have is the only truth and the only direction toward knowing who you are. You are designed to be observant and follow patterns. The patterns that the voice within is trying to bring to your attention will change you from the inside and give you the validation you've been seeking instead of needing it from others who aren't necessarily positive influences in your life. This can seem like the work of a lifetime especially if you have altruistic traits and tendencies. You may be someone with a sign on your forehead that says, 'I need a friend' or 'If you need something, ask me.' Folks will take these cues, maybe even unintentionally, and they will run with them for as long and as far as you have laid the track for them to run on. In some aspects it could be that they do know how to take advantage of you, and they use you on purpose without any intention of reciprocating. Regardless, many people will just move along with the program that you've set up for them, and it's important that you monitor your program and what you're putting out for people to read because that is what they will perceive about you. I've had many people that I gave the title of being my friend only to find out that they weren't really my friends at all. They were close associates who knew me.

What you call a 'friend,' you have to dictate. They have to know themselves well in order to be a friend to you. The person that you're speaking to: are they living up to those qualifying actions? If not, what are you going to do with that knowledge?

Act the way you want to be and soon you will surely be the way you act. Going back to the woes of my puny salary and big dreams—I was not being paid anywhere near what people thought I was making. I had always carried myself in such a way that led people to believe that I was successful and doing well financially. I guess that's what people refer to as having class. The truth is you are more than your neighborhood, you are more than the clothes on your back, and you are more than the people who you call friends. You are success personified. It's just the matter of making this instinctual awareness work and making yourself and your dreams more than just disconnected ideologies.

At the time I moved into my first home, I was so happy to take my three children from my first wife with me. I wanted them to have a lifestyle that was of a higher quality and safer than the experiences I had in some of the areas I had lived in. Around this time, I realized that I was internalizing ideas and allowing things into my life which seemed to match what I saw on the outside. Your lifestyle can be just as ugly as derelict streets littered with garbage and overrun by rats... There is a correlation.

By speaking with the mentor and owner of the house, it became obvious that I was doing too much to be accepted by others, and this was creating an imbalance within the nature of the care I needed to give to myself. These relationships clearly did not reciprocate my efforts and led me to stress and poor ways of coping. I was not being my best self in my relationship, and I was responsible for what had happened to make the marriage fail. I am a strong advocate of the idea that no matter what it is you need—the reality is that you need the inner you.

When you are a social person, who has grown accustomed to being extroverted toward lots of people, it can be difficult to get into the habit of being with yourself and really trying to hear your inner song. Since I was a young child, I have been surrounded by people. My role and position in life has always been within the areas of production and assisting people along the way especially when it comes to performing music. These arenas have always given me considerable and substantial amounts of joy. Nevertheless, when you're singing in the choir of life and focused on how much you genuinely love people, the way you spend time becomes a habit revolving around those you care about. Every person I've ever worked with I've cared about. I savor beautiful moments of life with people and this is just my way. It takes intentional behavior to take all of that love and care you've given out and apply it to yourself so as not to become unbalanced and out of order.

Sit down now and listen to yourself. It's okay to sit alone, spend time alone, BE ALONE, and really talk to yourself. I got something I want to talk to ME about. I don't need to go through no hocus pocus or light no incense. You see, I was made in the image of greatness... Everything I need is within me. I have always been a person that has totally loved God, but I wouldn't say, 'God fearing.' God is to be loved and adored.

He walks with me, and He talks with me and tells me I'm His own.

God loves me and hears me when I speak to Him. To fear Him would be to negate the fact of His divinity and omnipresence. Picture a man shouting at a woman that he is her husband or that he is her father, and she better do x, y, z, or else. I feel that decreases the value of what is real, true, and possible. Thoughts come to my brain—if they're good thoughts, it's God. I have to hear His voice calling to me. You know that voice: 'Don't worry about yourself, I'm going to take care of you.' The voice you try to shirk off like it is a delusion or fanciful ideation. The type of 'dangerous' thought pattern that could lead you to thinking things are really better than they seem. . .

What if you listen to this voice and follow its path? Will your destruction and disappointment be imminent?

'You be My arms and My legs, and you open your mouth, and I'll speak for you.'

Well, this is no farfetched fantasy. You *just open your mouth and make sure you're in My will.* People think the love their creator has for them is so clichè, but it sounds good, because it is good.

Long story short, I moved in on December 22, 1991. By the 24th, the house was covered in Christmas lights. In fact, we probably had more lights than all of our neighbors combined. From down the street our house glistened like a gargantuan ornament. My cousin Perry remarked, "Bobby, the pilots from JFK airport use your home as a guiding light to land their planes." And I believe they did. Not to mention it was Perry and his wonderful musicians who celebrated with us by coming to the house for all of my summer parties. When it wasn't summer they would cram into the lower level of my home and play music into the wee hours of the night. I really believe it was Perry who helped me develop my ideas for this wonderful property and turn it into all it could have been. Thanks, Cuz.

Again, here's how I manifested my marvelous mini-mansion: I would go by the property every day and sometimes twice a day. I would walk around the property and place my hand on either the side of the house or on a tree in the beautiful back yard. I would talk to the object I was touching. I would talk to myself. I would breathe deeply and allow my desires to flow forth and manifest. I also took pictures of the home; I strategically placed these pictures in the areas of my apartment that I frequented the most. As I walked around admiring the photos, I would tell myself that I was already there.

I even went shopping at a grocery store in my "new neighborhood" a few times. Once, I saw a friend of mine from Far Rockaway. "What are you doing here, Bobby?" she had asked, surprised. I smiled and replied, "I love shopping here. The produce is always fresh." I added that I would soon be buying a home in the neighborhood. At this point, I still did not own the house, but I spoke as though I did, and I shopped as if I did. I also remember getting my haircut in the next town over just to feel out the vibe more.

One Sunday in church, the pastor delivered a powerful message about how all things were possible. I received his message within the depths of my soul, and I ran with it. I went to the property, and instead of saying, 'I'm getting this house,' I changed my words to: "This is my house." If you want to manifest something great, there are a few things you must do. First, subtract the doubt. Subtract any friends that bring about low self esteem whether through habits or shared activities. You must surround yourself with like minded energy. This will propel the forces of manifestation to do its job. Bring on the good stuff. It's yours waiting to be released.

Next, clean your slate. Add to that slate those things that you desire. It's very easy to say, "I want–," however, that's not where you will go by speaking those words alone. After recognizing your purest desires, you have to transition toward exercising your muscles. They may be weak at first, but the more you put them to use the stronger they will get. In the meantime, sit back, and allow your beliefs to become greater and greater.

Now set positive intentions. My intention is to be helpful to myself and to others. Always remember that what we do should be done for a greater cause. Finally, I always tell my daughters this analogy about fleas, and I think it's worth repeating now. Fleas have the ability to jump 7 inches vertically and up to 13 inches horizontally. But if you take a few fleas and put them in a jar, poke holes in the lid, and secure it, the fleas will jump only the 3 inches that the cap allows. Now get this, when you let the fleas out of the jar they will only jump the same 3 inches they have been acclimated to even though they have the capacity to jump higher. The lid on the jar is analogous for the negative thoughts you listen to. It's the negative people in your life and the old familiar thoughts like: 'No you can't,' 'You can't have it,' 'You've been bad,' 'You don't deserve it,' 'You don't have enough money,' 'Your health is not the greatest.' These are all caps. Get rid of the caps and jump.

Once the lid is off, you're only halfway over the hurdle of healing your jumpshot. You still have to figure out how to expand your leg propulsion and leap higher than you've ever been trained to go. It's more than possible. It's your destiny.

I got the house! 274.

CHAPTER 2
THE CHINESE BAMBOO TREE

If you want to learn the correct way to grow into your greatness—hear me out: The first step is patience. The second is perseverance. You are worth the time and the action it takes to create the best version of who you are and the life that matches. The Chinese bamboo tree shows us the importance of taking time to grow. For one year it requires consistent watering, turning of the soil, fertilization, and, of course, sunshine. After the first year there's no sign of growth. This same thing occurs throughout years two, three, and four. . . Nothing visually happens. The trunk does not grow thicker. The leaves do not mature. The Chinese bamboo tree is seemingly a stagnated plant. Imagine the dismay of the ignorant gardener! This tree you attempted to grow evidently absorbed none of the nutrients you so carefully assisted in creating for it. All that time watering and fertilizing, and the plant gives the impression that it was all a waste and for nothing. Some would walk away, give up, and throw in the towel. Does that sound like anyone you know?

How many times did Edison try to invent a working light bulb? Every miss I'm sure was frustrating. There were, of course, naysayers in his life; people revoking their support all through his trials and tribulations. Edison never failed. He just tried 1000 ways that didn't work. All the while, he was getting better and better; likewise, in the first four years of the Chinese bamboo tree's life the stem does not show growth, but something pivotal is taking place below the surface. The bamboo tree is digging its way deeper and deeper into the earth in order to develop strong roots. Consequently, and after all of the cultivating during the previous years, the tree is prepared for its new cycle. Once the roots have taken hold and have grown formidable, within six weeks of the 5th year, the tree starts to grow.

Eat clean. Learn recipes that include vegetables and drink your water. Grow strong roots. Become a fixture here. Be immovable.

Sit down and think about who you are. The storm always brings heavy winds and strong torrents of rain. If you're not weather resistant and your foundations are not deep and strong, you will be tossed around even in the midst of life's most lenient tempests. It is not about what you are going through right now as everything is temporary. The constant is the mettle you are made of. Just sit down, and think about who you are. Some people don't want to do this until they're at an older age. They don't want to recognize their greatness, their resources, or the areas they need to improve in. There is no time to delay. We are not here to repeat the regrets of our forefathers.

'And the voice I hear, as I carry near, is no other than my own.'

The reason why your inner voice wants to speak to you is because it's been placed there. Sometimes it's yelling, and you continually put the lid of doubt on what's real. Your voice is the answer that has been begun since before you were born.

'Go and show My love to the world. And as you do that, I will bless you invariably.'

It is within your reach to be surrounded by good friends, safety, and live in a good home. You will be protected from dangers seen and unseen, and you will be blessed with things that you see and things that you don't see. You will be provided with things you desire and things you didn't know you were worthy of. Furthermore, we should embrace the time of unseen growth and use it to build our character, stamina, and discipline. In order for any building to stand tall and beautiful, it must have a strong and deep foundation.

The bamboo tree needs the first four years to grow long, strong roots into the earth in order to support its height. The roots spread deep and wide. This feat takes time while nothing apparent is happening above the surface. The roots take the longest to cultivate, and they will support the life of the plant as it grows. Once this initial stage has lasted its duration, the Chinese bamboo tree skyrockets; growing 90 feet tall in just over one month!

This same transformative process takes place in our lives as well. Sometimes it is necessary for us to settle and grow in the midst of our storm. Once our growth occurs, we too can soar high to reach new levels of greatness. I know you've been hearing a lot about keeping your body and mind well—there is a reason. People with love in their hearts have been dutifully working for eons to preserve knowledge and bring these very important messages, now being replayed for you in every aspect of life, to the forefront. Health and wellness, with the highest intentions and regards for humanity, are the biggest trends we are seeing right now across the board.

There is a major shift taking place and it's because of you. A message that's been passed down relentlessly for generations, from all walks of life—on repeat and only becoming more and more clear; finally, uniting people of all creeds and ethnicities. Someday, not too long from now, we will look back at this time period and realize how much we were learning and accessing together when it comes to caring for ourselves in the most righteous ways possible—ways that invariably foster nature and cause our environments to flourish. We are not only learning about healing ourselves but showing our loved ones and our neighbors that they too have the answer within.

When I started to get older, I was diagnosed with high blood pressure and diabetes. The doctor put me on so much medication to bring these two diseases to a normal reading. I remembered that when my mother passed away, she had a night table full of medication. My mother was a head supervisor at a hospital. She was head of nursing for 35 years where I grew up in Brooklyn. Her friends were all doctors, nurses, and administrators at the place where she worked. Yet with all this medication that was on her night stand, she still died. I know we don't live forever, but I also don't think God put us here for all of this illness and disease. The love of my life, Elaina, introduced me to a ministry that spoke on holistic healing without medication after I had gotten my diagnoses. At first, I could not fathom that healing was possible, but I knew that anything is possible if you put your feet to your faith. To make things happen, you have to move. You can not succumb to idleness and just sit down while expecting change. Rest is important. Rest when you need to, recover when it's necessary, get a healthy amount of sleep, but don't settle your life on wishful thinking; do something about whatever it is that is ailing you or nagging at your soul.

It's been 25 years since I've taken any medication. I found the answer, and the answer was within. I was putting too much inside that wasn't positive and not enough inside that was. I had to learn how to eat everything in moderation with lots of water and rest. I'm not one to go to the gym, but I don't mind walking 4 or 5 miles one evening or doing sit ups at home along with some breathing exercises. Oftentimes, we think that in order to make a change we need to take the most drastic steps. Don't make what's creating vitality in your life feel like a punishment. If we punish ourselves we may not be equipped to sustain what we are doing to counteract whatever it is we want to fix or change. Instead of deciding tonight to never eat a cookie again or to run three miles everyday this week, make one change today and see where that takes you. Continue making changes and adjustments, adding to your program, subtracting what doesn't suit you, and in 6 months you will feel a difference. In 6 months, because you didn't punish yourself, you'll be able to continue to go another 6 months on this path. It's up to you to begin, and it's up to you to continue with assurance even in the moments when you do not see any effects taking place.

I found my way towards supplements that could help you with your blood pressure and diabetes. These supplements along with following a healthy diet and drinking the right water served me well. It's been said that cancer, for example, can not live in an alkaline body. Your body's balance has a lot to do with what you are giving it for food and how you are processing the food. Nutrients are key to improving and maintaining important and vital bodily functions. How your body absorbs these vital minerals (vitamins) depends on how well your organs are functioning. Blood flow needs to happen just like a car engine needs to run. This is why so many people in our lives motivate us to get moving.

I believe in you. I know that all it will take in your life to get you active is for you to believe in yourself, know that you can do it, and know that you will feel better living this kind of life rather than being sedentary. The doctor said to me one day that my numbers were going down and that he was going to take me off some pills for diabetes. This same day, I went to my cardiologist and he said, "Mr. Banks, your EKG looks great. I'm going to take you off of some of these pills." Three months later, and three months of staying away from fatty foods, doing medium level exercise, and eating lots of vegetables both of my doctors took me off of everything. They said whatever I was doing to keep doing it, because I was doing great.

When my wife passed away, my sugar levels went back up because of the stress. I told myself I was going to fix it. Now both levels are where they need to be, and I'm getting good rest again. I had to learn to be good the same as everybody else. The most high has me here, because I'm in service to others and those around me. God told me at the age of 11 that I will have a long and fruitful life, and that I would outlive the majority of the people in my circle. Look at me, as sure as my name is Bobby, what he said to me has come and manifested in my life. I have been and still am living and going strong. He promised me to be a lender and not a borrower. I wanted to be able to be someone that people could go to for help, as a giver, someone who could hear the spirit, and someone who could also remind people that we have everything we need inside of us.

When you have all of this in your heart—I know you do since you are reading these words—you want to take it and give it to someone else. I'm not looking for self glory and self praise. I'm looking to be as much like this, so I can help people. Although the process has taken a long time to get my roots to hold, just as the bamboo tree needs multiple years to take to the soil, do know that once the peaking starts—the growth is exponential. The Chinese bamboo tree grows almost three feet a day.

In anchoring myself, I have found the growth in my life far outweighs the time it has taken. I am currently living without any stress, and I am medication free. My health is all in accord. What people think is not possible, is not only possible, it is probable. For myself and for you to live this way is what we are most meant for. You've suffered long enough, you have cried many nights, you've had many times when you've struggled, and now you deserve to live. Now it's time for you to reap the harvest of your labor. Let's make sure that the answer we have is not just lying dormant inside of us waiting for us to call it forth but that we actually utilize ourselves to our highest potentials. If we do not call our voices to the forefront of our lives, our abilities will stay inside of us to leave this world totally untapped.

Through my time of growing, I have experienced and learned many aspects of knowledge about myself and my truth. My time of growing has come to a pace where I can't even keep up with myself, and I'm sitting here still knowing that there is more to come. I challenge each of you who go through the reading of this book to be encouraged and to make yourself known for exceptional growth just like the bamboo tree.

CHAPTER 3
ABOUT ELAINA JOY SANABRIA BANKS

As I look back on these past few years, I'm more amazed with all that has transpired for me and in my favor. God has allowed me to celebrate 16 birthdays, 16 wedding anniversaries, and 16 of the most blissful years of my life with my best friend, Elaina Joy Sanabria Banks, aka EJ. Together we celebrated everyday as if it were the most special day of the year. Therefore, every day was Valentine's Day, every day was our anniversary, every day was Christmas, and every day was a vacation. Everyday we prayed together; either I prayed, or she prayed. I celebrated her in my life before we ever met. Unequivocally, she was my purpose and I know, without any hesitation, I was hers. All of this, in spite of the negative thoughts that went out and around town about why she wanted me and why I wanted her.

The talk was that this young woman was looking for some rich man to take care of her. The other side of the conversation was that I was looking for someone younger. The truth was that God had ordained my union with Elaina before I had even thought about it.

I remember when her family moved on my block. They moved two doors away from my house. Her younger brothers were still in high school, and they would work with me as I was planning McDonald's Gospel Fest. Their father Mike and I became friendly prior to them helping me. Our friendship began when he invited me to jog with him in hopes that I would join the church he ministered. One Saturday, we jogged past his house, and I saw a young woman

I had never seen before in the window. Our eyes met, and I felt an instant connection.

"Mike, who is that in the window?" I asked.

"Hey boy, that's my daughter!" He exclaimed.

Later that week, I saw this sweet woman riding a bike in a long flowing skirt outside in the street. She had a glow around her like the rings around Saturn. Her aura was so radiant and so star-like. Something internally just pulled me toward her. I knew that moment would head out to a lifetime. How it was going to happen. . . I didn't know. I knew that if this was the pull and order of God, He would work it out.

One day she rang the bell. Funny enough, I had just told her brother recently that I liked her. "Ooo, I'm gonna tell Laina," he chided. I'll never forget that. She came downstairs with us and we all talked. I eventually invited her to accompany me to a big concert in New Brunswick, New Jersey at the Jenkins Brothers' church, who were the hosts of McDonald's Gospel Fest. I invited her and her brothers to come with me. We took a limousine down to New Brunswick. We were treated like royalty when we walked into the church, because everyone knew me. By this time I had already fallen in love with Elaina, and we had never kissed.

She had no boyfriend, and I had no girlfriend, so I just waited until God said 'Yes' to us. The rest of that year we talked often, and I spent a lot of time around her and her family. The answer within, without a doubt, was that I had to follow the right way. I had to marry her. I told her father on New Year's Eve.

Elaina and some friends were at my home. I told her that it was time and that I had to tell her father. At this point, he had moved to Michigan and had been living there for a few months. I decided to call him on the phone right then and there. "Mike," I said after he had answered and after I had greeted him for the holiday. "I gotta tell you something, please listen to me. I love your daughter, I want to marry her, and I need you to know two things: 1. Your daughter will never want for anything and 2. I will take such good care of her, she will never be worried or concerned that I mistreated her." When I was done with my spiel, the silence on the other end showed that he did not want to hear any of what I was saying.

He had moved to Michigan earlier in September of that prior year. A little before that, Elaina had moved out of her house and into an apartment in Hempstead. Eventually, on one of his visits Mike came to my house. He was a minister, and he was very well respected—not at all a man you want to offend or disappoint. We sat in the living room and we talked. He was not rough, but he was not satisfied with what I was saying. He said, "If you marry my daughter, neither my wife nor myself will be at this wedding. None of her brothers or sisters will attend. It will just be you. None of my family will come."

I pleaded with him saying that Elaina had been a model daughter her whole life. How could I sleep at night knowing that the potential of us and our marriage could put a once happy bond into such disrepair? This was the family I wanted to be a part of. I could not be the cause of despondence between a father and his daughter. I could not be responsible for a family not having peace. I looked for the answer within, because the answer within does not cause turmoil. If the answer within does not allow peace to continue or peace to come, then you have the wrong voice giving the wrong answer. From January on, we planned out the wedding while Elaina had private conversations with her mother and some conversations with her father.

She told them whatever she told them, because I never asked her, and she never told me what they spoke about; but I do know that around March, her father decided he was coming to the wedding.

He was coming to the wedding, but he was going to sit in the back of the church. And by April, he was going to come to church, and he was going to sit down in the front, but he wasn't going to walk her down the aisle. Around May or June, he was going to walk her down the aisle, but he wasn't giving her away. Around July, he was going to walk her down the aisle and give her away, but he would leave right after with his family without coming to the reception. In the interim, I was not working on faith; I was working on knowledge, because if this thing is real then the answer within had to be undergirded by the power of God Himself.

I don't think biblical scriptures into my conversation, but I need to say that: 'The spirit beareth witness with our spirit that we are children of God.' In my interpretation this means that if I have the spirit of righteousness, and you have the spirit of righteousness: I don't need to persuade you, hurt you, or twist words around for you to agree with my ideology, because it's already written. With that, all I had to do was keep planning this wedding to make my bride feel good.

When I finally got the okay from Mike that he was coming to the reception, I called my friend Terrance. Terrance was a parent at one of the schools I taught at, whom I had helped make a few lucrative business decisions. Most people know what I do. I help approve people's credit for cars, and I help people secure mortgages for churches, businesses, and homes. Due to my strengths in negotiation, I have been able to guide people who would normally be rejected toward getting the cars and homes that they desire and the businesses that they long for.

Terrence and his lovely wife owned a limousine company in Bedford Stuyvesant, and one thing led to another when he and I first met. I found out he needed more limousines for his business, and I was able to assist him in securing two to three at a time. I told him he would make more money if he bought regular cars and then had them cut and fitted into limousines. Terrence ended up with twenty-five limousines and a few Rolls-Royces. He was *thee* man with access to a full line of luxury limousines that he rented out because he owned them all.

With Elaina's father's final okay, I pulled every string to do what I wanted to do. I wanted him to feel comfortable with his 11 children (from the same mother) coming to our wedding. I said to Terrence that I needed every limousine he'd ever had on the lot to be at my wedding, and Terrance gave me about twenty-two limousines and two Rolls-Royces, and my sister gave me one Rolls-Royce, her personal car. I made sure that Mike and his wife had a car, that his children had cars, and many of the guests.

When her family arrived at Bethel AME Church in Freeport, New York, and saw a 50 voice choir in Elaina's favorite color, red, they knew that this was her wedding just as much, if not more than it was mine. I hired Norma Bazemore to do all the interior decorating in the church, and she stayed there overnight for about 24 hours in total. We had an orchestra with strings, horns, and a harp. We had two pastors: Elaina's pastor, and the pastor of the church I was playing for. Brother Milton Brown and Pastor Harry White were from two different churches, and our wedding brought them both to the same altar.

If I had to speak about Elaina's pastor, Brother Brown, that would require a book entirely of its own. I had never met a minister that was so grounded, passionate, and scripturally based until that alone drew me to him and his ministry. The church Brother Brown pastored had a strict rule of their members not marrying someone from outside of their congregation, not to mention, visiting other churches outside of their denomination.

Elaina's church was very uncompromising, so for this man to come from his church to marry Elaina and I said a lot about the love he had toward joining us in holy matrimony. His support and participation allowed people from EJ's congregation to come to the wedding and the reception. Their idea was that it was impossible to make it to heaven unless you follow their premise. This wedding would not have been done for anybody else. Seemingly every principal, every doctrine, everything Brother Brown had preached for 50 years spoke against what he did by participating in our wedding ceremony. I say all this because you would think in order to have gotten them to rsvp to our wedding that I would have had to beg these people and gravel on behalf of myself and my bride, but I had absolutely nothing to do with their decisions. All I had to do was listen to the voice within, because I knew the answer was there.

The place was jam packed, the weather was beautiful, and Elaina smiled from ear to ear. When her father walked her down the aisle, it was one of the proudest moments of his life with his daughter. This was not how it started, but this is surely how the wedding went.
I had the wedding reception at the most prestigious of venues on Long island. It was called Leonard's of Great Neck. Even to this day, it is known for its beautiful halls and exquisite catered formal events. I didn't want another bride in the building that day. I boldly told the owner not to book out the other spaces within the venue. If anyone else called and tried to book another wedding on our day, I wanted them to say it was already reserved. They said all they could do was to try to keep the other guests away from our area if the venue was booked with another wedding. I said I didn't want anyone else in that building, and do you believe that we had Leonard's completely to ourselves? Mind you, this was during a month when usually the calendar was full.

We got inside Leonard's Palazzo, and there was nothing I needed that was not already there. The best part of the reception (even with all of the music, the dancers that I had hired, and the host that I had hired) ended up being the fact that everyone truly was having a great time, enjoying the atmosphere, one another, and laughing without there even being a drop of alcohol in the place. No one was drinking; not even people sneaking drinks from outside. During the wedding, Elaina and I left the hall to go to the suite and change into our special reception attire. We wore absolutely gorgeous African garb that G Marie designed and made custom for us. G Marie made the most beautiful African women's and men's clothing. Our custom made threads were embroidered, flowing outfits, with hats to match. The clothing was so astounding we didn't want to sit down in fear of wrinkling or disturbing the elegant fabrics. Luckily, we didn't do much sitting since we had over 200 guests.

We walked around the space as if we were king and queen. We floated on air conversing and greeting our guests. I noticed at one point three tables had got up and left. I asked EJ who those people were who had disappeared. She laughed, asking me if I had remembered how she told me she had invited some of her friends. Well it turned out that since many of her friends were still in school, and since some of them still even lived at home, they didn't have any money to put in the envelope! Oh well. . . They should have stayed!

So how did the wedding go? There I go again with 'The Answer Within.' Live and in Technicolor! Afterward, a car took us to Manhattan to a private location, and in the morning we were whisked away on a beautiful honeymoon.

What a relationship! I thought my life was full before her because of the people that I knew, the things I'd done, places I had gone, and the music in my mind; however, it was empty until she flew into my world and I jumped into hers. For, in the words of the Supremes, "My world was empty without you babe. From this old world, I try to hide my face, but from this loneliness there's no hiding place." I thank God for the two girls she left me to travel beside from place to place, to run back and forth to school for, to run behind and clean up after, to help do their homework, and to get up every Sunday and go to church with. Most importantly, I'm thankful I can run to the kitchen and prepare a homemade dish and not just peanut butter and jelly sandwiches.

Later on, it was also because of Brother Hunt, aka Chef Hunt, that I gained even more necessary culinary skills in the kitchen after my wife's passing. He would sit with me in his kitchen while I was learning my way around. He offered me some lessons on how to make a few dishes, along with his lovely wife, Sister Hunt—who gave me the 'Yes, you can,' even before President Obama. Chef Hunt and Sister Hunt were our gracious friends from church who assisted me when I needed help.

Thanks EJ. From our first meeting, we knew this would be strange, yet real; unusual, yet long-lasting. Our love is often talked about but seldom duplicated. Our little became much when we placed it in the Master's hands.

Let's rewind the story to before I met Elaina. Previously, I had been separated from my first wife for five years, and for two years I wanted to find the right lady to be with. I searched everywhere, and I began to write down on a piece of paper the details about her. Finally, when I met my wife, I said 3 weeks in, "Elaina, don't ever tell me you like me, cause we'll be married within a year." And we were married a year from then.

I wanted our wedding to be perfect. You might think this is a bit untraditional, but I took it upon myself to plan everything down to the invitations for her. My sister, Sharon, had to bring Elaina aside and tell her that I was not to be the one to choose her wedding gown. Truth be told, I had already had one picked out! EJ chose a wedding dress that completely stunned me when I saw her wearing it. Elaina came down the aisle that day during our ceremony, and she looked like an angel. I couldn't believe my eyes. Our wedding was so gorgeous that for years after, women would come to us to help them plan their weddings. EJ and I would sit across from them, sometimes in our home, and I would talk to them about how important the right venue and caterer were. EJ soon would have the conversation completely under her lead. I might have decided on the colors of our wedding, but hers was surely the spirit who had set me to work.

EJ gave me a new life to live. I thought I was preparing her, but all along she was preparing me. I thought I was teaching her, but she was teaching me. I thought I was showing her how to do so many things, yet she was showing me. Because of EJ, I'm able to raise my two daughters to be all they can be and more. Because of EJ, the three of us are able to walk in the light and share the light with others as we navigate through our lives.

I told EJ that prior to our marriage, I wrote a list of the requirements I had for my future wife. I even wrote how I wanted her to talk to me, how much we would respect one another, and how we would show respect to our children. I told Elaina later how I had wanted someone I would only want to talk to like a queen and who I would show respect to at all times. My deepest desire for my future wife was for her to never have to go through what I went through. There would be no way that we would fight or argue and speak negatively about one another. I had come to realize the mistakes I had made in my past relationships, and I would never again take myself or a loved one down that path. Most importantly, the person I was praying for needed to have a relationship with God that was paramount and not just a Sunday lip service gal. I showed her the list after our first wedding anniversary. I expressed to her that my list was nowhere near what God had given me in her. I was touched by an angel. Mya, Belle, and myself are all the better because of the day EJ was brought into this world. Thank you mom, Sheila Sanabria.

It has been six years since my wife, Elaina, and I had the privilege to express our love to each other with words, deeds, and honesty. My entire life has been changed, and I am forever grateful to God for marching me toward her path. Where would I be today had she not said, 'Yes!' against all odds? Our relationship went from gossip to glory, from no invites to crowded tables of happy families, from getting marital advice in the pastor's office to Elaina counseling other couples. *Cuando vuelva a tu lado.* "What a difference a day makes."

Just the thought of her still brings her fragrance to my nostrils and a smile to my face. The times we shared together have given me such a delight. The "sugar plums" are still "dancing in my head." I could not have asked for anything more. Without cessation, I prayed for over 5 years for the ideal person to marry. I wrote it down and saved it. I vividly remember sharing the actual piece of paper with EJ years after our marriage. It was titled, "What I wanted in a wife…" It was shocking to see all that I received with EJ that I did not write down. I missed it by a landslide. What she brought to the table was categorically more than any mere words I had ever penned.

It took God six days to create the world and all its living things. It took God one try to put Adam asleep and make him a woman. Finally, it took 47 years for God to usher his handmade vessel, Elaina, into my life for multiple purposes. She was my personal life coach, my guide for fatherhood, my way of being an example husband, the teacher of honesty and integrity, along with many other attributes. Today, I am still amazed as to the life I live because of the life she lived. Not to mention, I now can make more than peanut butter sandwiches.

The last meatloaf I made astonished me to see how my girls got up for seconds and thirds. In the words of Walter Hawkins, "I'm Not The Same." Had Elaina not entered into my life, I would not be where I am today. Somebody said I wouldn't make it, a few people said I couldn't take it. . . Look at me: I assure you without any contemplation or reservation, I am eternally and happily a servant to God for what He has done though EJ. God didn't just put a beautiful face here to spread His holy word; Elaina had an equally beautiful heart.

As we experience each moment in time, it is highly probable that we take these moments for granted. Think about it—how often do we stop and give our love and appreciation to those near and far? Let's stop and express love and appreciation for those that we cross paths with. The people that make life worth living are all around us on a day to day basis. They could be the faces of people we lock eyes with on the subway or pass while driving down the street. They could be the people that we just aren't too sure about or even those who seem to make life a little more difficult, adding a layer of complexity that in the moment we might not understand or be so easy going to accept. The people around us, whether cruel or kind, harsh or loving, make us better versions of ourselves every single day. Love looks different based on what we need in order to get us home. If the person didn't come against you, how would you have ever found out your true potential and nature? If the gentleman in the sports car next to you didn't test you on your patience that day, would you have been so apt to bestow even greater patience to the little child in your care? Even our so-called "enemies" love us. Without them, we wouldn't know the truth, and we wouldn't be able to find our answer within.

We should always treat each moment as if it's the last—for we never know when that moment will be no longer; turning yesterdays into memories. I witnessed love personified through EJ. I observed how she touched so many people in so many ways. She would give instead of lend. And yes, she always had more to give. She loved God, her husband, her children, family, friends, acquaintances, and our church. There were countless days I saw her reach out to strangers. Before we knew it, they would be in our home having meatloaf with our family. For several years, we had a few people come for Thanksgiving dinner who could barely speak English! One year in particular, she had been out shopping at a thrift store earlier that week and came upon a loving mother and her children. Elaina gathered that they had newly immigrated here from Portugal, that they didn't have family here, and she invited them to our home.

It got to the point where my sister asked me, "Bobby, who's coming to Thanksgiving dinner this year and what language do I need to study so I can be a little more fluent?!" Fortunately they understood our smiles and welcoming gestures. I could not stop Elaina, because this was her ministry.

Every moment of your life is a moment for gratitude. It's not always easy to find the aspects of life to be grateful for in moments when it feels as if you are unable to catch a break. Things may seem a certain way to you right now. I know you can think of times in your past where you might have said: "But Bobby… gratitude? This just can't be," but there is always a reason. Trust yourself and the power of your love so you will be able to look within and find the answer. She stayed married to me for 16 years. And when I showed her that list with everything on it she laughed, because I had written that my counterpart was petite and small, and she felt she did not live up to those expectations. "Ha!" I replied. "EJ, you stomped all over this list." I told her, "You are 1000 times better than anyone else in the world, because you are you, and you and I were meant for one another."

You see, my life is geared for me the way it is geared for other people. Life is geared for you.

When my wife died her brother, one of her 11 siblings, told me that they would phone the house everyday after we got married to speak with their precious sister. They would call seemingly to make small talk, but they were really calling to make sure she was doing alright and that she was content. He told me this just after she passed away, and he said that there was never a doubt in his mind that EJ was happy, loved, and cared for. I told her father before marrying her that if he would just breathe easy, his daughter would never want for anything.

There's something better than drugs and sex: a pure relationship. My wife has been dead since October 2016. It's been 7 years, and not a day goes by that I am not grateful for our marriage.

He will be your guide. He will be your guide for how long? Even unto the end.

I remember vividly the night EJ left us. She was playing on the floor with our two girls. She and the eldest rolled around on the floor as my youngest leaped off the bed. It was around 9:30 p.m. on Sunday evening.

About an hour later, EJ had prayed with them and got them settled into bed.

We spoke for a moment and said goodnight with love in our hearts. Several minutes later, I heard a sound coming from her. I thought she was talking in her sleep.

"EJ, are you talking in your sleep, girl?" I whispered.

She grunted.

I rolled over and began my journey back to sleep. Fifteen minutes later, I was awoken by a hard thump. I bolted up. To my dismay, my wife had fallen to the floor. I immediately leaned over her and checked her vital signs. They were all good.

The next thing I did was speak to God on her behalf. During that time, my daughters were calling 911. That was all good.
By the time the paramedics came, I had settled in my heart that our relationship would be good no matter what. Our love for God, and our love for each other was all good and intact. No need for last minute apologies.

Today, it's still all good.

Is it possible for us to love some, yet hate others and call ourselves friends of EJ? Is it possible to love your creator, whom you've never seen, but hate those you've laughed with, broken bread with, and have enjoyed one another's company with? Those of us who carry a load of malice, hatred, and ill-will bring illness to ourselves. Moreover, we win nothing. At what point will we reach out and 'touch somebody's hand?'

Stop, and release your negative feelings. Show love and appreciation of the time we have with those near and far. EJ demonstrated that it is possible to love—even those we do not like.

EJ has given me that which I have searched high and low for. I have found it. I sit with a void that has not been filled. I have eyes that will not cry. I make music that brings joy to others but will not ring within. But this I know, this Joy—Elaina Joy Sanabria Banks—that I have—the world didn't give. The emptiness of Elaina Joy not being here lets me know all things are possible, because for 16 years that emptiness was actually filled with the greatest love I have ever felt. I will not allow anything to impede the knowing of what I had: God's most precious gift to me. Let's stop and really show love and appreciation of the time we have with those near and far.

On the anniversary of her departing—with a smile full of accomplishments, with no regrets, and with no need to cry or scream—I am at peace. I do not need lovelessness or loneliness. Nor do I need to run. I am not in need of an apology, and most importantly, I have no need to look for God to correct any wrong which has occurred. I am at peace. I have forgiven all. I am forgiven. I say, let us all carry the spirit of love. Let us all strive for more apologies and even more forgiveness. For then, and only then, shall we begin to live a full life.

With that, things are going so well for me and the girls. So in loving memory of my wife, if I have wounded any feelings today, if I have walked in my own willful way, if I have caused one foot to go astray. . . Let's allow this moment to be our newness.

CHAPTER 4
TRUST THE PROCESS

Seven or eight years ago, a gentleman who once came to do some work at my home wanted to open a restaurant, and he spoke to me about some of his desires. As we spoke, I shared with him that he needed to write the vision to make the claim. He stopped in awe to listen. I told him the things he really wanted to have were within his reach. He had never owned, worked in, or operated a restaurant before; however, there was a pulsating force that would not cease nor would his stomach and taste buds take a break from craving the bursting flavor of his barbecue battered beef with black-eyed peas. He told his lovely bride of his inner desire. With a small amount of savings this became a respectable and relatable, day-by-day, month-by-month, operation of *trusting the process.*

Several months later, he and his wife moved into the neighborhood of their choice and purchased their first home. Not long thereafter, a restaurant became available several blocks from their residence. Ten months later, after finding the answer within and calling things as they are—with all licenses signed off and filed, all the plumbing and gas hooked up, with no demolition needed and renovation complete, he was a month away from just an idea coming to fruition! Yes, a thought became a beautiful restaurant. Funds did not equal the job nor did experience match the assignment. What was needed was a mind, a mission, a bottle of BBQ sauce, and extra chairs for the grand opening.

So how did he do it? Number one, think about including your

goals into your daily life habits, whether physically or mentally, as doing some extra work. These changes and shifts need getting used to before they are fully integrated and we get to see the major fruition of our dreams. To the untrained eye, the sudden changes and shifts can often go unnoticed, or the doubts and negative mindsets can sneak in outweighing the positive perceptions. This may lead people to become disillusioned prematurely.

Before you give up on yourself and the positive shifts coming your way, while your dreams are actually manifesting, think of how you got used to anything that you didn't always do so effortlessly. For example, if you take on a five pound weight and you go on living life holding that extra five pounds, at first it's going to be noticeable, but naturally, as with anything, you grow accustomed to it. Now that extra five pounds, that at first was difficult to carry around, you don't even think twice about because you've lifted it continuously. You have increased your threshold and your life is different; you're moving faster on the five pound tasks in the world. You can more easily execute your will with such facile victory as you have never quite managed to do before the development of your muscles.

Next, you go for something that weighs nine pounds, and you work at lifting it once. Boy, is it heavy. The first few times you're dropping it. You lift it 4 or 5 times. Nothing changes at first, but soon after that you're now strong enough to handle that twenty-five pound weight you've been staring at collecting dust in the corner. You're able to reach this newness, because the last weight started to feel like a feather. Why, you can even carry them both at the same time!

Look, the beginning is going to be difficult, but finally you're going to lift your life wherever you go, without thinking. When you see twenty-five pounds now you know you can lift it. You don't need faith, you need knowledge.

Every time I fail, you know what I say? I say, 'Thank you.' Every time I make an error, I have to say thank you, because I know I'm one error closer to my success. I lifted that twenty-five pound weight 13 times, and when I attempted fifty pounds, I dropped it. I couldn't lift it after 10 tries. Each of those 10 tries I was smiling as the weight dropped to the floor. Each time I falter or come near, but still miss, I am as happy as I can be. People think I'm crazy because I'm happy during the ugly process. Is it ugly? Or is it magnificent to know that you're just one step closer to achieving it all? Failure is necessary. It is going to happen. I know this because if it takes 30 times to do something, and I'm at 27 tries, I just know I'm just one error closer to perfecting it. I use the same illustration in my life. I use knowledge and I use algebra. I don't need to use faith which is why my faith has increased tenfold. Knowledge that is learned, analyzed, and expressed by the answer within has given me no reason to doubt or fear.

Make your thoughts, your words, and your desires so big that they almost feel not in your realm of possibility to even manifest—just speak and know. Many people say, 'speak and believe,' but let's simply begin with "speak." Understand that 'no' is not an option: "knowing" is all there is. As you embark, and without a minute bit of hesitation in your thoughts, know the resplendence of the journey ahead.

How many people are carrying an idea around that is ready to be birthed, but they will not allow brightness to permeate from the inside out to the surface? Why carry that weight? The process cannot and will not manifest itself on its own. However, it does not take the 'Know All Handbook' or the mega-funds to make your desires happen. It takes an idea and a starting place, even if you don't have a plan. Everybody has inside of them a level of greatness that needs to be sparked. When you find the spark of what interests you most, you realize it's the thing inside of you that you already have. Your natural gifts, talents, and skills, which you had already when you were born, are meant to be sharpened and fostered. Just like when we go to school and our courses are meant to help us embellish our gifts, life will also give us experiences to sharpen the tools in our tool kits.

The graveyard is the richest place in the world when people die with untapped gifts. Some of us have all that we need inside of us but never use the abilities intrinsic to our life forces. Ideas which could have cured cancer or have cars floating in outer space have all been stagnated. The thought bubbles are gone, invisible, suspended, and floating in the ether. What a pity would it be to go through life with ideas in our heads and witness the graveyard become rich with these dead thoughts. In college, I wrote a paper entitled, 'Walking Dead With a Heartbeat.' Man, that teacher flipped out! "Mr. Banks, where did you get that idea from?" The English teacher excitedly asked me about my paper one class. "You need to develop these thoughts! Walking dead. . . With a heart beat!" She was taken aback by the concept. I put those two ideas together based on how people are living and walking around this planet but yet they are dead, because they won't budge on making any movement toward their futures.

God told me on multiple occasions, for a variety of ideas, to get paper, sit down, and start writing what's in my head. He assured me that He would send people my way for what I needed in order to reach my destinations. Keep lifting those weights. You're not alone, and someone who's also been lifting is traveling toward you right now. They're the people who are going to do it for you. They could have the empty restaurant, be the lucky man or woman, or be the person hiring you to produce the event. Do it for you, because all the people who said they would set you up and help you out didn't. They weren't supposed to at that time. That is okay. Celebrate instead, because you're three people down the line and, therefore, three people closer to who is going to be that breakthrough force to push you through with them to the other side of where you were to where you are meant to be. Oops, there it is!!! All the people who didn't help you or who weren't the people for you—you can't look back and hate them. They did their best. They were taking you to the person who is meant to and who will be best suited and aligned for you; the same way you are for them.

Now in my later years I can say I've become so bold that I have actually become an oddity to others. I have to tell you something though. . . I won't walk around telling anyone I am going to close a 200 million dollar deal. See, God told me to stop telling people my success stories ahead of time. Turns out, people don't always like to hear you're lifting that fifty pound weight! I'm not saying they're necessarily going to stop you from lifting—like 'poof' the weight has vanished and your gym membership is revoked—I mean that it doesn't feel good for you to tell someone good news or something you're holding out for and have your conscious or subconscious mind realize that they don't want to see you win or that they carry so much self doubt that they can't see you win since they can't see that win for themselves. Carrying that type of realization in your psyche can take up space in your mind and become a burden. As someone who has always been enthusiastic about the accomplishments of others, it can be rather daunting to know that the people who you adore, even if they adore you, can be bitter enough that they don't realize their shade of green or hue of blue can actually sting your eyes when you're looking straight into it. Sometimes it's best to sit on your nest egg and wait until it hatches for you in private. Be selfish! Keep secrets!

You don't use faith as much as you use knowledge. My faith is my knowledge. My knowledge is that it will happen. So I don't even use faith anymore. While I'm praying, God puts an angel on the run, and before I can finish praying, the things I am praying for are already done. I thank God for things in my prayers that I don't even have. I thank Him, because it's not about my faith anymore. My knowledge tells me that I am so assured of His caring for me that my faith is now knowing I will be taken care of. I think this way until I see the foundation for what it is. I don't use faith; I do use knowledge. Some people say how can you please God without faith? I know, irrevocably, that God's got my back. So at this point, faith becomes knowledge: knowing. I'm not saying faith is not present. I am saying my faith has gotten so deep that it becomes knowledge. I know that God has my back. I know that when I do right by Him, I am on my way toward my destiny. I have gotten so successful in acknowledging what faith can do through God. Because of my laps of victory, and because of my growth in things that seem impossible, I have now come to my realization that faith works! My faith has been so deepened that now it has been transformed to knowledge. If your thoughts are flowing right now, use this opportunity to take time to find the answer within yourself, and share your views in a journal or on a piece of paper—your book could soon be coming down the pipeline.

Write your vision and make it clear. Don't weigh your options—there are none! There is only movement forward. If you muster up the tenacity to move into your mastery, the desires will manifest. Inside each of us there is a level of greatness. Bringing it to the surface requires a spoken word: A word of confidence. A word of authority. A word of declaration.

As you speak it, know that the universe is steering it your way. For the answer, my friend, is not blowing in the wind—*the answer is within.*

It's very important that prior to the consideration of making your move towards financial wellness, happiness, and success that your conscience and your heart are clean. They must be clear from any negative thoughts or ill-wishes toward anyone else.

Once you have achieved this level of love and gratitude, the next step is to make sure that you are conscious of the purpose of your finances. Your way of living must be, and should be, for the greater good.

Now, you are ready for your abundance to overflow.

CHAPTER 5
SPEAK LIFE

It's okay to talk to yourself. It is great to possess the ability to tell yourself that it's going to be fine. When life becomes dark, you have to know that you are the light. You have the answer within. Use it! Speak with power. Know that before you finish speaking the things you speak of are already on their way. Nothing can stop the inevitable.

The question is: how? Wake up with a 'Yes' on the bottom of your feet. Former President Obama shook the world with three little words, "Yes We Can," so perhaps you should continue to reiterate the same. We are the 'We,' in that sentiment and we are the 'I'. Always say, "I can." Remember that as you speak, as you walk, and as you move around in the morning to start sending out your greatness. This way when you leave your home, your victory has already gotten a head start on running toward you. . . Morning by morning, new victories.

As you speak, walk in faith and in assurance. This manifests the newest version of you. Give no apologies for success. If you're not the recipient of the greater you, who will be? I remember walking around almost on my tippy-toes in order not to allow my greatness to shine. I was apologetic for success at work. What better way to show our greatness than through all of our complexities? Shine. Smile. Sing. Don't apologize.

When I was a youngster, the profanity in my everyday vernacular was sickening. What came out of my mouth makes me shudder to think about now. I had the capability to use a broad range of vocabulary, but I was complacent in my rebellion and sounding like I had no sense. Every other word was 'F' this or 'F' that. I was raised in the church, yet my mouth was dirtier than a dog's. I had to clean up my act. My tongue was the same tongue allowing me to speak softly in life and never have to feel pressed or desperate to achieve and unlock my greatest gifts and potential.

On behalf of my answer within, which was always speaking to me with such grace (even when it was yelling at me to do the right things), I needed to learn some self control and discipline when it came to the power and connotation of my words. These changes might not seem big to some, but they played major roles of importance to me. Everything in its time. I couldn't be the man who met my wife or who learned how to be a great parent if I never molded my outer self into a greater version of what my inner self told me I was. I was chipping away at the excess granite in order to sculpt the better me. I wanted to give my daughters a better life. We all went to a church that didn't allow any drinking or smoking. I wanted to keep myself as clean as possible. I also wanted to do everything I could to make my wife feel safe in this new relationship we had.

I ask God everyday to make me an instrument of His will and for whatever He gives to let it flow through me. I speak life, and so I assist Him in aiding life to live. Through my years of studying and research, I have noticed that many people would rather look down upon you because of your failures rather than looking up at you because of your success. My friend Stanley Brown once told me, "Bobby, bad news can be your good news. Do what it takes to keep your name in the right place, for the right reason, and at the right time." Speaking life is imperative for your self growth. Do you know that with your inner conversation on stand by, you can preserve many years of your life? Why give away years of your life when you simply need to encourage yourself to be a better you? Don't carry any extra baggage, especially that of which does not belong to you.

Don't accept any negative, toxic, or filthy words from anyone. The outside negativity can retard your thought process.

We use such a small percentage of our brain. We cannot ignite the greater portion if it is filled with goo-gob. Don't apologize for working on you while others are working against you. In the words of Frank Sinatra, "Massive success is the greatest revenge." Joy, unspeakable joy, is the way.

You must know that not all storms come to destroy your life; some come to clear a path. In the words of Warner Wolf, the New York and D.C. broadcasting legend, "Let's go to the video." This reflection device is in all of us. It must be utilized in order for our metamorphosis to occur. Once I began to rewind my video and review my experiences, the practice enabled me to take my life to the cutting board and cut out people and things that did not contribute to the greater me. My video review protocol is so strong that it's practically automated. As soon as I walk out of a place or event, everything I did comes back to me to the point that I can see and hear everything that I have to do better. I can extrapolate everything that needs to be tweaked and refined so that I can be the best version of myself. And the good news is—it's in color! I can see every part of the playback. Once you let the playback come, and act upon your reflections and realizations, you will be so amazed at how you can grow and become your truest essence.

Many men when it comes to relationships that end badly she-bash their ex-wives or ex-girlfriends. I can not stand here and be blessed while telling a lie. It is usually the man's fault or the man has a lot of contributing factors. There's things that have been done that I would never do as this new man that I have sculpted out of myself. I had learned manhood from what I saw other men do, and in the beginning of my first major relationship, I took my examples from the wrong people. I caused my relationships not to flourish or bloom as they should have. I stand here to tell all of my male friends that the true value of being a true man is to be responsible to your family and to yourself. In the words of Shakespeare, 'To thy self be true.' My first marriage could have been a much better relationship if I had been a better man. Debbie, thank you for being with me during the process. We all have to learn from our own errors so that we will not be caught going on in circles again and again.

Once we can captivate all experiences that we've had in our inner video, we can get a true overview of how to speak life in a greater way. Let me give you your first assignment in this additional new way of thinking. Sit still and think of that thing that needs to be moved out of your way (let's not start with the Mediterranean Sea or the Canary Islands). Now begin to find inside of you 10 reasons why it must go. Write them down. On another page, write 10 ways in which your life will improve once this movable obstacle is gone. Now visualize yourself helping others in a better way without it.

The main issue that people have with motivational techniques is that they try them for an hour or a day and then they give up. Once that happens, you are further back from where you started. You must have persistence, tenacity, mastery, and the will to go forward. Remember, the thing that must be eliminated will not leave on its own!!! Kick its butt hard! You have to be so careful with what you say and how you say it, because your inner voice is hearing you. You have to be able to tell the difference and distinguish between what voice you are hearing and what message to tune in to. You have to check your wording and make sure that it's the best for you to have a smile on your face and a brighter day.

Having the reserves I need on hand, which allow me to serve people, makes me have a better day. When my wife was alive I told her, 'Elaina, when you feel good, I feel great, because my life is here with you and making sure you have the best of everything life has to offer.' When I'm blessing other people it's like an amoeba; it splits itself and takes its own shape.

Speak with conviction… not hope.
Speak life… not desires.
Speak greatness… not fear.

Write your vision. See the end result clearly before you get there. Don't allow false education to appear real—that's FEAR. It must not exist in our way of thinking and mastering. Continue to check your lists. Check them twice. Start to speak the good and watch the bad decrease. Write the increases and gains you are making. Next, watch your ideas move mountains.

For the 2019 spring break, I took my daughters to Greece. We went to a small restaurant inside of this very large library. We did not like the menu or the service, so we left. As we were making our exit, we envisioned a better place to eat. One of my daughters suggested that I call a driver to come and get us. We walked out of the building and there he was. His name was Demetrius. We greeted each other, and the rest is history. He knew Greece like a C Major Scale. For the rest of the trip, not only was he our driver, he had become our concierge of all things Greek; all it took was speaking with authority. This happens so much that now I get flustered if my desires are not in my hand before I finish speaking. And, guess what? Now Mya and Belle are trying their hands at it; they can see that it works!

Yes, I am a strong advocate of speaking with confidence. I no longer speak with wishful thinking. I now speak with experience. It is my experience that enables me to see my heart's desires traveling right my way. Just speak it!

CHAPTER 6
ABOVE AND BEYOND

Many people live so far beneath their inheritance and it feels good there. The low place is comfortable, because the place where your goals are set is based on your present reality. Even your dreams are regulated, suppressed, and stifled because of your state of mind. You can be in a place of being complacent and not even know it. Looking around all seems well as far as your natural eye can see: being grateful for the job you have, while being subject to verbal abuse at times, dealing with the premise of letting 'good enough' do, looking at your bucket list of fun in the future tense rather than drinking from your cup now. It's an inner mindset. As you think, so you are. I'm sure you've heard that before. My belief, however, is deeper—it's more than you think. Everything is based on your inner knowledge that propels itself into an outer fact. Therefore, you may not fly literally, but those things you seek? For goodness sake, they can, and they will fly to your destination.

We must stop, look, and listen. In order to begin this process of going above and beyond, one only needs to *stop*. With all of our day-to-day routines that slip into months and sometimes years, one must stop and look around.

Look within.

Pull yourself away from yourself and be on the outside looking at everything that makes you, you. While looking at yourself, start to write what you see. You'll soon see the inevitable rat race.

Write thoroughly and fast. I know that sounds like an oxymoron but write. Continue to look deeper into your present place in life. Look at your friends, places you go, what you shop for, what you eat, how you dress, and what you watch on TV.

Examine your spending habits. These writings can be several 10 to 20 minute sittings. Once this data is compiled, start to arrange it in order of your new life. Look at who you are, where you are, and what you do. Recall the last two vacations you took and how far apart they were. Consider how often your family eats together, what type of conversations are happening, and if there are any phone calls and texts not included that you wish were. Take time to dive into yourself. Please look closely at your friends. Look at who brings what and takes what. Look at what enhances you and what depletes you. Be sure your circle is filled with people who are lifting you up. You don't have to be the best or the greatest, but look at your next level up and out. Look up from where you are now to a place you've never dreamed of: a place outside of the circle you are currently in. Repeat this every day. Feel it before you see it.

When I was a young adult, I was drinking heavily and although I was not an alcoholic, my desire to transform myself and my life caused me to recognize that the way I was living was not the life for me. In order to meet my destiny, I had to realize that self preservation was the key to infinite growth and expansion. Humans can feel elated with life experiences and at times so very invincible in our bodies; we may not perceive any dangers. The possibility of destruction or the effects of chasing happy memories and good times in repetition, while using substances, can be looked past and ignored. Some habits can lead to, scientifically put, cellular degradation. In order to achieve my goals, I have to be confident in myself. This confidence and resolve lends itself to many factors including looking and feeling my best. We are our harshest critics and can often be the first people, through learned behavior, to deny our worth or feel doubtful of the odds required to see our greatest accomplishments be actualized.

It's much easier to be negative against yourself when you physically are not functioning well due to how you are fueling your body. The truth that sets us free is that we can only envision meeting our accomplishments head on because they already belong to us. All we have to do is respond to this truth and calibrate in order to align with the inevitable joy ahead of us.

I had to start thinking practically and doing what was needed of me to move forwards. Many people are close to being functional alcoholics the same way I was, but I knew that this potential label could not be part of my success. There was no room inside of my being for both self harm and self love on the road I was on. I had been given the experiences necessary to choose the brighter path for myself; knowing instinctively on the other side of this decision was everything God had meant for me. On July 3rd 1986, I said to myself, 'I will not have another drink, and I will not smoke another cigarette.'

Everyone at the 4th of July event the next day was waiting for my arrival and to bring the party so to speak. I said 'No' to my past self, and I said 'Yes' to the self who had grown in knowledge and experience. That day I told my friends that I was not drinking anymore. My statement was met with their laughter. I had stopped cold turkey and said, "That's it, I'm finished!" I took all the booze in my house and threw it all out. Once the alcohol in my house was in the trash bin, I took a shower at 6 a.m. While I was in the shower, I said to God, "Lord, allow this water to be synonymous with Your blood that has cleansed us from our sins."

What works for me, works for me, and I am sure you can and will find what works for you. Now over 30 years later, I have not had a drink or any other substance since that day. There were days over this sudden stop when I was tempted, but I heard a voice within saying, 'This habit and I can not live in the same house.' I chose to be the vessel of God's love over any external and illusionary effects—it's either your dreams or this.

This virtue to myself helped me raise my last two children. My way of parenting them included the mottos: Whatever you see me do, you can do. Whatever language you see me use, you can use—I wanted my life with my two girls to be based on the idea that whatever they saw me do, was good for them to do. What they could say was based on what came out of my mouth. I know other people teach differently. You do as I say, not as I do, for example, but I'm telling you what worked for me in my house. Why not check my daughters and check myself at the same time and let us all grow into our greatness? My way of doing things was not forced upon my two daughters. However, a stop sign on the highway, for example, works most of the time. Boundaries and rules do give us the requested and mandatory advice needed. With that, when you pour in your best ingredients and a little bit more, all you can do is wait for those biscuits to rise.

Now it's time to listen to what your new self is saying to you. This is done away from phones, people, and music. These steps are life-changing and must be worked on with passion. You will know what, who, and which things need to be extracted from your life. As you enter the better you, be cognisant of your surroundings; every round goes higher and higher. Watch and enjoy your new circle. Not everyone will go where you are going. Remember that it's okay to part ways, even if you don't know if it's for a short time or a lifetime.

Dinner should start to be different when your family eats together. As we know the kitchen is usually the place where most people gather and spend time with one another during holidays and family times. Can you imagine the stories and topics that will come out when you are sitting at that table beaming because of new found peace and happiness? I cherish the times I sit down with my family. Growing up, dinner time was a special time in my house with my sister, my mother, and my father. It was a time to talk and laugh at corny jokes and share lasting memories while sitting there at the dinner table. All that matters is that you and your family are sitting together in fellowship with one another. The answer does not only come from within so to speak, now it spreads out and around the table.

Conversation topics will be different and grow to new levels, because the people at the table will not be the same. You can take that one of two ways. As with family, think of it like this: when someone else in the room begins to grow, their growth will trigger everyone else and be transmissible. If you expand your consciousness and thinking around being alive, naturally, so will the people who keep up with you. Hopefully in our case, the growth triggers us to have better quality topics and discussions with those we love and not a situation where people no longer see eye-to-eye. That's where your knowledge comes in. You know you love those at your dinner table, because you know you love yourself, and more than that, you know how much God loves you. Your table is set for just the right people at the right time.

Be good to each other, and you will see the blessings exceed your expectations. How does this work in harmony? Well, the answer within tells me that if I point at you, I'm pointing at myself, because we all have room to grow; we all have room to grow to a whole new level. In the case with family, it's easy to take those relationships for granted and feel so frustrated with the world that you're okay with distancing yourself and even cutting family members out. In some cases our own children or parents could be distant from us and treated like strangers. In situations such as these, we need to examine which finger is pointed and in which direction. Sometimes in this growing process the parent or the child can be on the other side of the equation in cases when they are not having a good relationship—is that their fault and not mine or my fault and not theirs? We are trying to make sure it's not us. Therefore, we need to go forth and make time to probe as to the cause and the reason for all the reactions and dismay. This whole new level of ourselves is what the famous and inspirational, Les Brown, speaks about when he says we are growing into our greatest selves. In the words of my mother-in-law, Sheila Sanabria, one night when she was advising a young mentee of mine, she told him, 'Remember, when you point one finger at me, you're pointing three at yourself.'

Late one night, I was at home watching television when an infomercial came on the screen. It felt as if the man on the screen was talking right to me. His message that I had the power within me to change my life has never left me to this day. The man presenting was Les Brown, one of the most notable motivational speakers in the world. I have grown and expanded on his high level way of thinking and, in turn, so have the people in my life—our love and power really are the gifts that keep on giving.

Les Brown's tapes were written back in the 80s. They were cassette tapes made to order and they were advertised globally. Due to his command of words and unmatched ability to speak right to the heart of what troubles humanity most, his message led to the betterment and wellness of millions of people. His famous position on self improvement is that we have the ability to recondition our minds. When I was struggling, his tapes were the catalyst toward being on a road of self healing with help from within. I noted that all of his books pointed toward the idea that the answers and power we need are within us. The things I have gotten from him have helped me and touched the lives of folks in every nation across generations. We all have something in common that unites us. None of us connected by the answer within will ever let ourselves stay and remain down at a level where we feel sorry for ourselves because that was never part of our life plan. I knew then, just like you know now, that my best days were still at hand.

When Les Brown's tapes were starting to take their effect on me, and his lessons were helping me to hit strides that I had only dreamed of becoming accustomed to previously, I had to call the number included with the tapes. I left a message expressing my gratitude and desire to speak with him. It was impossible for him to reach out to everyone who called him. He was not only at this point a national treasure, he was 'The Motivator' and internationally known. What bounded Les and I seemed greater than the call and my message. I felt that we both had the same star guiding us. I knew I had to make that phone call, and he knew he had to respond.

Sure enough, after a few days, the telephone rang. It was Les! I shared with him the countless amounts of concerts I had produced in the metropolitan area, and I shared with him my ideas. His wealth of knowledge had to go outside of the TV commercials. I told him I would be instrumental in aiding his message to get across to the masses. He accepted my invitation and the rest became history.

I might be considered a great motivator by many, but I am nowhere near the phenomenal Les Brown. Many people reading might not have heard of him before reading and now are on their way to search his sold out shows on YouTube. Some of you may not have even been born when I was watching those tapes, yet you understand and know his message. We are all currently tapping into the compilation of Our Greatest Hits. We are all brothers and sisters walking up the highway to the brightest version of ourselves. If I can rest on the fact that I helped to share this great message of the power within so that nobody, whether you're my friend or friend's friend, or someone reading this book would ever need to go deeper into lowness, such as struggling with drugs or helplessness, depression, becoming hooked on vices, etc., then we have all fulfilled a great purpose; not only just myself. Les Brown's motivational teachings instruct us on how we can pull ourselves up by our own bootstraps. He along with many others nudged me in the right direction. How many great motivators in your life have nudged you? We are never alone.

Your family in spirit are here in the flesh. In other words, you're on the right side. Since we are here, and since my testimony is based on all of this being true, well then—there is no need to mope or be sad, because we can reach out and know that things are possible.

It's already been done for us. You own the truth, and the truth has and is still setting you free.

My mother Jessie's favorite song when she was alive was, "If I Can Help Somebody." The lyrics illustrate a person's life who is fulfilled, because they share the essence of their being with others. "If I can help somebody as I pass along. If I can cheer somebody with a word or a song. If I can show somebody he's traveling wrong. Then my living will not be in vain." I motivated myself by moving forward from here on out saying, 'Wherever I am, or whatever I do it is never my last stand.' —Whatever I do, I'm always going to help others. If I can help others then my living will not be in vain.

My mother's house was a central place where people gathered when she was alive. Then everyone started to get married, and we would eventually only see each other at funerals. This really affected me. I wrote a letter to all of my cousins and their children that I read to them during my eulogy for the last of my living aunts, my beloved, Aunt Norcenia Moore:

Do you remember when we looked up to all our Aunts and Uncles?
Now, we are the Matriarchs and Patriarchs of the family,
We have a responsibility to give Guidance, Advice, and Help with problem solving to the younger ones.
Help to give a better understanding of the word of God and so many other things that our family may need.

We all bring a multiplicity of Ideologies, Philosophies and Literary Interpretation to the table
We all bring different Strengths and Weaknesses
We all bring different Gifts and Talents
We all live in different Neighborhoods, Cities, States, and Countries

We all enjoy different Restaurants, Foods, and Desserts
We all Vacation at a plethora of topographical points

We all Worship in different Buildings, with Different Choirs, play Different Music, and have Different Ministers

Yet! We still are all One.

Let's always treat each other with Respect and keep Laughter at the forefront of our Relationships

Love ya,
Cousin Bobby

I didn't want that funeral service to be the last time I saw my family, so I was able to envision the message I needed to relay and concisely speak to those who needed to hear it. My mother is the glue that bonds my family. She still keeps us close from her place in heaven. I help her by furthering her legacy. You are a valuable person in a line of succession also. Your loved ones, whether they're still here or passed on, desire for you to continue their truth and create something that is a testament to their love.

Jessie Banks, my mother, was a mother to countless people, and I saw how she helped others spiritually, mentally, and financially. She had been a blessing to people in and outside of her family, and she never gave up on those who were her immediate relatives. She was supportive of everything I ever wanted; even before I wanted it—I would get it. My giving spirit comes from her. I take joy in giving like she did. The act of assisting someone else propels me. My mother would always say you have to share, you have to give, and not to be a fool, but if you have more, give. She told me that it will anoint me and be like oil in my life to help me move through and flow. My mother instructed me not to make these gestures publicly or humiliate those we were helping by making a spectacle or boasting. She said that just by being the blessing that I am to her and that she was to me, I needed to be that to others, and I would be on the right path. If I could help somebody as I passed along, if I could show somebody something I learned through my traveling, then my living shall not be in vain—that was her motto and that became mine as well. 'You need to learn to share,' she would tell me. She would sit me down and say, "Share and give, and be blessed." My Christmases were bigger than anyone's Christmases I knew. I didn't know any family that received what I received on Christmas. We had 3 rooms packed with toys, bikes, and one year a quadraphonic stereo system. Everything I wanted she bought and this was her pattern. She worked hard and did well, so she showed us kids how our work ethic could amount to a world of abundance and joy. "When the cousins come over you better share, boy! She would call out. "Don't set this stuff in a corner. You better share!"

I have successful people in my family. My sister has a doctorate from Columbia, and my brother-in-law is a real estate tycoon. I have medical doctors in my family—one thing they all have in common is that they have never stopped trying to unlock their greatest potentials, and they continue to strive to be, as Les would say, their 'truest selves.' Yet we never get to a place where we are satisfied so that our conversations will always grow and so will our children's intended conversations with their friends and family. My nephew works for the President of the United States, my other nephew is an established renowned choreographer who has produced dance routines for Beyoncé and the like, my youngest daughter is developing her writing ability for lyrics and aspires to work in the music industry, my middle daughter is majoring in theater, and my oldest daughter has gone to one of the top highschools in the country, Brewster Academy, and now is a flight attendant. My sons, Chris and Brian, are entrepreneurs working in the transportation industry. My oldest son is also an entrepreneur. The fact of it all is: the better someone does, the better we all do. Even the people who you have distanced yourself from are now better for having known you, and vice versa, as you are for having known them. We each carry a new and improved way of being ourselves from simply existing around one another.

Always set the rules by your example. You can lead a horse to the well, but you can't make him drink. However, you can run that horse around that track until he begs for water. You may just have to get your running sneakers, because you are operating above and beyond! In the words of Patti LaBelle, "I've got a new attitude." Your walk and talk will open doors for you of which you have never imagined. Just keep your eyes open and watch things come your way that you did not even have an inkling of before.

In order for these rhythms to flow and continue to flow, you must have genuine love as your bottom line. Growth should never be for the purpose of vindictiveness. Your power should always assist you in the assistance of others. This action alone will perpetuate itself. Love conquers all. Love pulls you up. The bottom is where it is most crowded. Move away from the crabs. Their job is to pull you down. Incessant downward tugs will become absolutely unacceptable as you begin your upward travels above your wildest imagination and beyond anything you could ever fathom.

My life has been a life of giving and that's why I hurt so deeply when people steal from me, because you don't have to steal from me, ever! I'm a giver, and I will give you more than you need. And so when people say you're a Christian, and you need to forgive and accept people back into your schedule. . . I say, if God has something to tell me I don't need anyone to interpret for me. I can walk around and not hate you. I can even walk around and know I'm sending you love without having you take up space in my thoughts. People are allowed to move on. If a person steals or lies, I won't be able to work at my best, so I won't be able to be around them. I can not function at my best around liars and thieves, and therefore, I'm no good to God.

Your reality is influenced by changing from the inside; it will indubitably transform your outside. People can grow and have room for forgiveness. Reverend Doctor Clarence Norman Sr. told his congregation a powerful message from the pulpit one day about forgiveness and how the ability to forgive is for you and your glory— not for any sake other than your own. He said go in the dresser and take out that momento you've been keeping back there as a reminder of the hurt and pain someone has caused you, and throw it in the garbage! That dresser drawer can also be a metaphor for what you're holding on to in the back of your mind—people's faces whom you barely even know but received an unjust gesture from. They don't have to live with you in your house for you to be a Christian man or woman. "It's only pain," the reverend said. "Throw it out. Why are you holding onto it?" We should not hold on to the anger, the pain, or the agony any longer.

Letting go and surrendering to loving those who have wronged us and forgiving them in our hearts is for no one else but for us; and for nothing else besides easing the burden of carrying these wrongdoings on our soul. It doesn't mean we have to do anything other than wake up tomorrow with the light back in our eyes.

CHAPTER 7
THE MUSIC NEVER STOPS

Living on Long Island is a totally different experience from Brooklyn and definitely Manhattan. Knowing EJ loved the city, I wanted to surprise her with a gift. We went into Manhattan often. We would stroll down the busy streets, observing people, vendors, and cabs as we talked and shopped. Knowing that she would love to have an apartment there, I spoke it into existence. She gave me her usual glare of validation and reinforcement. She trusted me whole-heartedly.

Rule one: 'Speak with Knowing—Not Hoping.' Then, leave it there. Don't beg, plead, or be repetitive. It's on the way.

I was in my office and a client came in and requested my services. After a bit of laughter and small talk, I looked over her application. I noticed that she handled apartments in a luxury high rise building in Times Square. The rest is history!

It is known that the average person has six degrees of separation between them and any person in the world. I believe those six degrees of separation do not apply to me. I'm too resourceful with the people that I know. Today I have 3500 contacts in my phone from all walks of life. When I'm selling cars, I sell to politicians, rap artists, gospel singers, choreographers coming back from being on tour with famous artists, and people from the church. I offer people in my community assistance with mortgages, because my contacts are on the board of the bank. All of these people together help me decrease my six degrees of separation down to two. It could be sickening to have this much power, but I do, and I use it!

Many of my friends know that I'm a good conduit for assistance between their cars, homes, furs, and events. People have come to me practically my whole life to do what I am still doing to this very day. Just Ask Bobby Consulting—I never started the company officially, but since I was 14 years old people have come to me and asked me things. Anywhere from, "What do you think of this?" or "How about this?" to "Can you help me with this?" I always oblige, and I am grateful for the people I know. That one person can really make a difference and by connecting people with others a spark can ignite and rock someone's world in the best ways possible!

My family had the privilege of using Times Square as our backyard. With all the hustle and bustle of the area, we would notice people walking around with their headphones in and smiles on their faces; totally oblivious to the sounds around them. They had turned us off and put their music on. With that, I say to you, with all the obstacles in your way—find that center, and allow the music to keep you balanced. Tune into you, and shut the world off. A great exercise in this area is to first realize that if you don't take yourself away from the magnetic pull of things in your life, you will become part of them. You are not your bills. You are not your husband, wife, or child; you are not your employer or colleagues. You are perfectly designed to be you. The best part of you is *you*.

I vividly remember a so-called friend of mine, who always called me his 'buddy." He went looking to get approved for credit but kept getting denied, because his credit was so poor. I guess he was hesitant to allow me to do what I do. . .

Before he came to me, he went looking for help on Queens Boulevard, next he went over to Jamaica Avenue, then to Long Island City, and a few other places. None of them could get him approved.

He finally called me and asked me if I could help him to get credit for a car. I told him I could give it a shot, so he came to my home and we engaged in conversation. I got some information from him, and I told him we would talk tomorrow.

Once you look at someone's credit, you can tell exactly what they've been doing and all the places that have already denied them along with the dates they were rejected. I know he waited to call me because of his shame. So here I am knowing this, going to my bank, knowing they will know this too, telling them how this person is my friend, talking him up, and saying how great they were. I was immediately laughed at. How is your "friend" going to go to six other places where they rejected him and have you put your name out there for them when they obviously called you as their last hope? Well, from six rejections to a brand new car, the journey for this client was one filled with failure and desire until he allowed his personal embarrassment toward his credit to be put behind him— that's what led him to an unexpected victory.

Yes, his story was bleak because of his enormous disrespect for his own portfolio. His hope of driving a car seemed more like a distant fantasy. Every attempt to secure approval had resulted in heartache and frustration until he tried one more time and had the breakthrough with me.

Since I was a kid, I've done what I've done: pulling up my contacts, making my phone calls, and making it happen. I've sold more cars than the average salesperson who works in a dealership. I've helped more people get secured loans than some banks have. It's all about contacts. It's all about the answer within. My friend is now driving a brand new car for himself and his wife to enjoy in their new marriage.

Reverend Ike was a minister who also spoke about the power within. His unique and overwhelming success allowed people to walk out of the church feeling their own level of personal satisfaction.

He often spoke about not looking for the pie in the sky, because you could not reach that high to enjoy the taste. He had a church in Washington Heights on 175 Street and Broadway, called United Palace. Working under his assistance allowed me to grow. I was injected with the ability to have unusual success. He had musicians that played much better than I did, but he saw something special in me. He was a people person, and he had an awesome ability to get folks to listen to him. Before church would start, I had to be down in the pit at around 2:25 p.m., because the bell would ring at around 2:33, and the door in the pit would close while the motor would start; causing the pit to rise up to the stage level. As the stage rose, the band that I was hired to lead would begin to play.

When we were playing at stage level, Reverend Ike would come out in his suits: powder blue, teal green, white. He wore exquisite clothing with paired scarves, and he had a beautiful array of fine jewelry; not to mention his heavily processed hair always laid impeccably on his head. He did not speak often about Jesus but more about the power within. Nevertheless, he would somehow always turn it back to God. He was an oratorical master of scripture, science, and logic. He knew the power inside that could turn someone's story into another level of their success. This guy was worth 3 billion dollars, and he trusted me to reinvent his pulpit and his stage. He loved my business attributes, he loved that I was a promoter, and how I had the ability to get stars to come and perform at his church.

My title back then was 'New York's Promoter,' because of all the successful concerts I had done. Ike needed my expertise around him. His heyday was in the 60s, and when I knew him it was towards the end of his empirical reach. To him, I wasn't just a musician. I was one of the best promoters in the city who was able to move things around and create more life at United Palace.

Ike had sixteen Rolls-Royces. One time while in Miami, Florida, I witnessed him buy four dress shirts for $5000 dollars a piece. People hated him for his lifestyle, because they thought he was greedy. Ike was eccentric. All my life I've always been ushered toward people with the power of success, toward people with the power of greatness, and toward people with the power of giving. I was able to see first hand from prosperous people, such as Reverend Ike, that the more I give the more success I have.

What he gave was the power of true hope. Your reward for living piously is not only received after you leave, but you can have a piece of your pie right now while it's still warm and out of the oven. He said, 'Here, reach out and get it.' This message caused people to give immensely to him; not only because of his motivational techniques, but because they felt compelled to assist him in spreading the message around the world. People across the country and the world began to sow into his ministry. The public doesn't realize the money it takes to run an empire. Ike had one of the largest buildings to maintain, and a staff to feed and pay as well, so he had a lot of funds coming in but also a lot of funds going out. People spoke negatively about him, but they were not aware of the expenditures to keep the payroll rolling, so to speak.

People speak negatively because they may not have what the next person has, but it behooves all of us to monitor how we speak about others. It's very easy to speak badly about them, but it doesn't feel good when the shoe is on the other foot. He who has not sinned shall cast the first stone. When you get to a certain level of success, you don't know how you're going to make decisions when it comes to your assets and your reach until you get there and experience it for yourself. Supporting people's small businesses and keeping life within your communities takes funding and resources. Without people like Ike, many lives and entire families would not have been able to be a part of an important outlet for growth. Think about how many college tuitions get paid within one year of our lives. Money must stay in circulation amongst people who walk among us, not over our heads. If you opened a new business, you would appreciate a customer like Ike.

I am very cognizant of what I say and how I say it. When you speak the answer within, that answer, just like your shoe, can't be tight. What is it that stops you from saying, "Oh man! That's beautiful, look at them! They're going here. . . He's going there! Wow!"—and really meaning those sentiments with pure enthusiasm and sincere happiness for others? Is it because you're thinking, "Why not me?" What is standing between the 'why' and the 'not'?

The answer is within us. We don't have to always bask in other people's glory, neglecting our own. You have your own story to write and tell. The more you take hold of the pen, the closer you will be to genuinely feeling glad for others. Knowing this one simple question does wonders. Ask again; this time in a different way. Say, "Why not me?" Because in all honesty, why not you? The people his church reached gave him their hard earned money, because they believed in his message and the power of his wisdom. Were some people upset with this? Sure. Why not them though? Why not you? Why can't you say, "I am diabetic free!"? We have people coming off of medication all the time. Why can't you? Where is it that says only Paul can get the answer that caused him to up and move and not to be in a sorrowful state any longer? Why did you read about Elizabeth Taylor, for example, being an alcoholic and doing whatever she did to heal herself, and not rhetorically ask: "Why not me?"

I sometimes sit and ponder, wondering is life really so unfair that only those we read about are the ones who bask in the glory? Why can't you be on that path too? From Paul, to Elizabeth, to John and Mary. . . Stick your name in! Write your name in! Stick your name on it! Write the vision and make it plain. **You** write the vision.

I love Denzel Washington and if he is on one side of the glory, what is the difference from him to Paul, Mary, or to John? What happened to Obama? Were not the odds against him? From Bush to Obama—why can't you stick your name on the other side of 'too'? 'Too' is a small word, but it brings an immense blessing and it can bring everything BIG into your life; big meaning yours.

This is a great time to be alive. Look around and see people who have decided to be themselves. Why not sing? Yes, you! Sing yourself out of trouble. Sing yourself free from the blues. Sing yourself to that place that renders you joy. Not just in the shower—sing! Sing a song. Sing out loud. Sing out strong. Sing of pleasant things, not sadness. Sing with jubilation, don't be mad. Just sing away troubles and sing yourself happy.

There is a song in each of us—the one that just comes to us naturally. Do me a favor and listen to The Staples Singers hit, "I'll Take You There." The music in your mind is sweet and resounding. It electrifies, stimulates, and motivates. There are a plethora of great 'songs' from great 'artists' and they are one thought away from being written and played—bringing you to your center. Know that the music never stops. You should keep listening! Why trade your hit track for the mess that did not make the charts? You are too good to be in or to stay in a scratched, broken, and discarded soundtrack.

Now is the time to enjoy the feeling of freedom. Stay away from being wrapped up and tied up in other peoples' misery. Tune your inner radio to your new station. Let your style of music play, and dance like no one is watching, because your music never stops.

Many times we need to recognize that we need an outside source of help that will stand up regardless of what is at stake. Countless friends, celebrities, and people could have left way too soon in my view, I believe. They had not been around the right people in their circle saying: "No, this is not good."

Let me tell you a story about my friend Will Bogle. Everybody needs a 'Will Bogle' in their life. When I was living on Long Island, on Coventry Road in that first home I purchased, this guy would call me all the time to arrange a sit down meeting, because he wanted to find out how to get into the music industry. I finally allowed him to come over, and we sat for several hours discussing. He seemed to be in awe.

Our conversation was very lively. We went from my living room area to my office. He liked my wife, Elaina, and he was a pleasure to speak with. Initially, when he entered my life, I was thinking he had very little to offer. Lo and behold, within six months I had hired William to welcome me on stage at one of my productions at Madison Square Garden. He knew that I had the ability to grant him numerous opportunities that could alleviate not only financial burden but also cure his inability to network within the industry he had so desperately wanted to be involved in. I would be remiss not to mention that at many moments during our relationship he shared certain views that weren't so pleasing for me to hear. I kept him on board and began to realize that the things he was telling me always came true. I thought to myself, 'Wow, this young man is really something.' Thus I began to let my guard down. I found him to be the most honorable, trustworthy, and truthful person. He carries an array of knowledge in many different areas and avenues. This helped me so much in my quest of keeping 'Bobby Productions and Management' on top. He said to me once, and I'll never forget his words, "Bobby, you are not the number one promoter in New York, you are THEE promoter in New York. Stop lessening your attributes."

His counsel meant the world to me, however there were times when he would come right out and say, "You are wrong." I was responsible for his pay check and any bonuses he received, yet he never allowed that to hamper his view or his answer to where I was or what I was about to do. This yielded in me having undying respect for him.

If you had a 'Will Bogle' in your life then you would tend to not make some of the common errors we are all faced with. Be a 'Will Bogle' to yourself and keep your eye out for when one comes along knocking at the door to be your friend. When William introduces me he always tells people that I am responsible for getting him started in the industry. He stands on my shoulders. He has traveled the globe, not just to Europe, and he has worked with secular, as well as gospel, talents. He is now a homeowner of a beautiful property and married with a beautiful family. I call him when I need advice. So, I'll say it again, if people had someone like Will Bogle in their life they might move forward with less tension. I've seen him take artists from making $1,500 a show to growing their income to $25,000 a show. In the words of Kurt Carr, 'I've seen him do it.'

Many people will not tell you what's right or what's wrong, because they're afraid they'll lose the connection with you. I wish I could have been Michael Jackson's confidant, Mike Tyson's right hand man, Whitney Housten's go to person, or Prince's leaning post, because there were things someone like me could have said to them beyond them paying me the millions. I would have said many things that probably would have cost me those millions of dollars and the job, but I still would have said them.

Think about the times in your life you have had to be this voice for someone when they did not want to hear you. How about the people in your life that you might not have wanted to hear? Maybe later on someone would nurture that truth a little more and it would click. Still, too many people left the world too soon, because they didn't have someone speaking truth to them. We must always strive to surround ourselves with the right people who give us the right influence. How is it that a person who makes millions of dollars hitting the lottery, in less than 2 years, becomes flat broke? A year later, they're on welfare after being awarded millions. We have to make sure to choose the people around us that know how to say 'no' to what we are doing at risk of being fired or put out of the circle. Choose people that will still tell you the truth. That's me. If you ask me if it's green, it's green; it's not blue. If we're going to let the answer be within us, then let that answer speak the truth outwardly, always.

When God speaks to you, listen to His voice. He knows you. He said even if you make your bed in hell that He would be there with you. He followed me, but at some point I had to turn away from the direction I was headed and face Him. That's when we began our walk through this life together. You know the voice of God. Your faith has to become unshakeable.

We work in knowledge, and knowledge is just another level of faith. If you have the faith of a mustard seed, that's all you need. Now, imagine you have the faith of an appleseed, and what if you have the faith of an avocado seed? I know when my caller I.D. says 'Spam,' it's the same thing as when things come down the pipeline of life that are not correct and are not for me. I know when it's 'Spam' and that if I pick up the call, whoever is calling me is attempting to have me going in the wrong direction. Going the right way means I need to find the answer within and listen to what that answer is saying. Once you know the voice within is listening to the voice of God, you can continue onward by providing your own soul with fool proof caller I.D.

Keep going, it gets easier. You'll get the hang of how reliable you are when you're telling yourself to either answer the call or ignore it.

CHAPTER 8
GIVE ME A CLEAN HEART

Many times, we look at ourselves, and we begin to feel uncomfortable with how things are going in our lives. We may be worried about our health, our finances, and even the state of our relationships. As we are faced with these calamities and hardships we wonder, why me? I say, why not you? It's got to be somebody. But with that, which way do we go? How can we make it through? We need to start learning how to focus on the 'why.' I'm here to attest to the fact that the reason for all of our broken relationships, poor finances, and bad health comes from the state of our hearts.

How many times have you looked at something and told yourself you wanted to get it done, but it's still there because sometimes we can be dead to motivation? The first thing we must do is follow through. Write down ten things you want to do and put them in order. Next, ask yourself which ten things are most important to your life. It's a sad thing to see how we have so many ideas in our heads that are the strongest and most important, but because we are so distracted, we won't put the finger of life to those tasks that will shift us into a higher gear. These tasks that could be life altering go on arrested inside of us for weeks and weeks. Bring out your best, and make this week be the one that changes your months ahead.

Before one can speak of greater health, greater finances, or a better relationship, you have to make sure you clear yourself of anything— and I mean anything—that is not pure. You have to walk around personifying love. You must forgive those who have wronged you. And you want to forgive them not just because you want to have power, but because you need to have freedom. Freedom allows your words to flow in a greater way. Free your heart from anything you do not favor.

One might ask, 'How do I find favor with myself?' If you can sleep at night knowing that you have given and done your best, you will feel favored. When you realize you can have all you desire, you will begin to find peace. Begin by giving love, even towards those that don't reciprocate.

Don't get me wrong—this is a very difficult place to be, but there's nothing wrong with it or you for finding this space challenging. You have to speak about life to other people. You have to speak about finance to other people. You have to speak joy, life, and laughter unto others. *You have to be the one to bestow positive energies.*

If you're like me, you're always helping. If you're helping, you're like God. He doesn't tell me what not to do. It's His love and security and that is audible. It's your voice as much as it's God's. Number 1: I'm not one to be an asker, my method of prayer is thanking God. My prayer is simple and to some it is almost offensive. . .

"Thank you God for waking me up and giving me the right time to do exactly what I need to do and leave the house."

"Thank you for the exact time I am meant to get into my car and drive this hectic metropolitan route. Please help me in that traffic we all know so well living in the tristate area and to be patient with everyone on the road."

"Thank you for giving me the strength and the will to focus on my day and where I am going, so when I walk into that school, I am a bright light to my colleagues and pupils alike."

The power of the words comes from the power within. Sometimes I do take it for granted. It's a part of me, it's not magic, and because it's a part of me, and because life can be distracting and move unpredictably, I can't forget to regain my posture and recenter myself. Don't forget to build on the resources you have to be grateful for. Where you put your thoughts is the product that will multiply. As I give, I'm blessed, and as I'm blessed, I give. It's a cycle because of the answer inside of me.

I vividly remember having a friend. I knew he could be a great person. For some reason, however, he had envy in his heart because of my gift of music. He was uncomfortable with my status in life and was even jealous of the relationship that I had with my wife. His negative feelings hindered our friendship.

In a case like this, you have to make sure that you don't go to a place where you become vindictive. You have to figure out how to feed into the betterment of that person. This will help you avoid anything that will tilt you or take you out of your center.

So, I gave friendship and spoke love to the person. Eventually, they didn't seem bothered any longer. Today, they are doing well, and my powers have been strengthened simply by giving my love to another person.

Your life is designed for you. There will be times when you come across people who haven't figured out how to decipher the writing on the wall for themselves. They become green with jealousy, and they're unaware their subtle or not-so-subtle gestures, facial reactions, and words, or lack thereof, give them away. Stand in your knowing. Their choices to sow discomfort or show unappreciation toward you by withholding well wishes or congratulatory remarks do not change your trajectory or the destination to which you are headed.

My mother was extremely well known when I was a baby. She was the president of one of the largest missionary societies in America. This enabled people to know and respect me as her son. My mother's first name was Jessie, and I was known as, 'Jessie's little boy.' Everyone admired me when I played piano at such an early age. I was 6 years old when I started playing, and by the time I was 11, I was already playing in churches. I took piano lessons from and studied under Maude B. Taylor, who was the chief musician at Cornerstone Baptist Church in Brooklyn, New York. The pastor there was Reverend Doctor Sandy Ray. This church was one of the most popular churches in the country.

My mother at the time was the head nurse at a hospital in Brooklyn, and she would work from 11 p.m. to 7 a.m. so she could be with us kids during the day. When she would get home in the morning on Saturday's, I would leave the house, put myself into the same cab she rode home in, and I'd go to my piano lesson. During the week, she would sleep during our school hours. My father would work in the daytime and be home all night.

As a result of becoming so talented, when my mother started a private choir in our home, I was in charge. My mother didn't know when someone was singing out of key; I could hear it. I was 11 years old, and these people looked at me like I was 11 years old. When I spoke with my high pitched voice, this lessened the credibility even more so. The music I had inside of me; they couldn't comprehend the level of what it was and what it meant. What I had in me was coming from a higher source.

Jesus was out with his mother and father in the village one day. When his mother and father left, Jesus wasn't with them, and so they went looking for him. They found him amongst all the rabbis in the synagogue asking and answering questions with people gathered around. When his mother and father found him he was teaching adults. They were astonished that at 12 years old he was teaching the

Hebrew priests and that they were truly interested in what he had to say. The rabbis and priests listened to the knowledge he brought forth to them. Just as Jesus did in the old testament days, so do we see children doing today. I'm not trying to take credit for what I had; it was just inside of me—I knew not what it was. It was a burning pulsating force that encouraged me to move forward into music and caused people much older than me to stop and listen. I might have been 'Little Bobby' on the outside, but I was 'Big Bobby' on the inside.

You can't put a judgment on someone based on their age. You can't assume the adult has all the information in the same way that we can't say, 'Because you're a child, you know nothing.' A child could have abilities that far surpass an adult. I was packed with music and these people didn't want to accept it. I was walking around at 11 years old speaking like an adult. I knew that this stuff was in me. I knew it, and it flowed out from the source like rose petals on a gentle, well fed river. It just flowed; my music has always been this way. I have no doubt that my best years are still in front of me. It's always been that way for me, and it is the same for you and your talents and attributes. Own them, and kiss your elbows everyday that you are you!

When I was a young kid, I was an anomaly for a few reasons. At the time you might think you're an ordinary kid, but I bet on some further reflection you start to realize how much you really stood out—send a lot of love and warmth to your child self. When I was an early teen, I loved the WMCA station on 550 am radio. Listening to this classic rock station and hearing these good guys talk between songs about all the music and the artists totally inspired me to know about secular music. I had the yellow WMCA sweater with the round face on it, and everybody laughed at me. I was the only kid listening to the classic rock station. I loved rock and roll and RnB, and of course, I also loved jazz: Cecil Taylor, Sara Vaughn, Chick Corea, and Miles Davis. I loved gospel artists such as: The Caravans,

The Clark Sisters, Hezekiah Walker, Donald Laurence, The Winans, Commissioned, and so on.

The adults around me were all looking at me like 'Little Bobby,' but I was as old as them in my abilities and tastes. I knew harmony. My piano teacher told my mom, "Jessie, he's not going to be a classical musician. He's going to play rock and roll and gospel." I was on the piano seat at 9 years old saying, "You can't do this, there's more to music than Rachmaninoff, Beethoven, Chopin, and Brahms!"

My voice was high. I was skinny like a toothpick and too small to command the audience how I wanted because of my size, yet I was poppin'. I did the lead scenes, I played the piano, I taught the harmony, I did vocal coaching; everything you could think of—I did—and that's why it's always been a part of me. As a music teacher now, I can teach two songs in a single class period and laugh. It's not that I'm great; what I do genuinely is how I express my love to the world and it pours out of me.

Do I feel good all the time? No. My peers, and my students don't even know when I don't feel well, but I keep doing what I do and I feel better. Sometimes people dislike the love I have. They throw rocks. I step atop those stones and I say to myself, 'You can throw me inside the ditch and pour all the rocks on top of me and all the dirt, and I will keep on climbing myself out. Not only will I free myself, but now there's so much rubble in that ditch that I am standing a few feet higher. Now I have a mountain, and you built it for me. All I had to do was walk my walk and climb higher. I was in the valley before they threw their rocks, now I'm on the mountain. You put me here. How did I get to where I am? You threw the whole quarry at me and made me a mountain.' I say to the people who cast stones but know not what they do: "I appreciate you and all the ills you throw in my direction." You will learn to do the same. Use the pain for your growth and other people's growth, so we can enjoy life with our families. Be grateful for not having to mine those stones or carry them all the way home yourself.

My participation in the choir essentially was just me playing my role and doing my part—a role and a part no one else there could have played. My mother was 33 years old at the time she had me, and everyone involved in her choir was around her age or in their mid forties. We would go to prisons and nursing homes, and we would sing for people all around the metropolitan area. I was 11 years old and telling women thirty and forty years older than I what to do, how to sing, and to use their vocal ranges. It seemed I had arrived and didn't know where I was going.

I was always in charge, popular, known, and respected musically. I've never been downtrodden because of my music. Music has always kept me healthy. Everyone has their thing. You know what you have. You know how it shines in your life. I'm not here telling you that you're not special while putting myself up. I'm telling you—if you know you have something then lean on it, and use it to keep your life upright and on a positive trend going forward. Have confidence, be a go-getter, and claim it.

By this time of my childhood, believe it or not, I was sought after by quite a lot of pastors and singers because of my skill. Therefore, it was nothing for me to handle my mother's choir. They trusted that I had the ear and that my feedback was genuine, because they felt the sensation one feels when the harmonizing is on point and reverberating throughout their body as a kind of heavenly feeling and susurration. And as far as 'play' is concerned, that was play to me. I did not need to go outside, because I could not play basketball. I could not play stick ball. I could not play handball. I just loved playing the piano at that point of my childhood and that's what I did. I did what I loved.

It's always good that you can have something that you can lay over your life; something that you own in your heart of hearts that can grant you access and open doors for you to make things work. I've never been totally down and out for the count in my life, because I was placed in positions where my skills developed naturally and this is the same for you. Be creative with what you have been through and experienced. How can you put yourself on or seek assistance with what you have developed practically just by existing as yourself? Personally, I don't even know what racism is, because while I have been faced with issues through everything I did, I remained strictly concerned with all that was working right in my life, and because of this I was always respected. I don't think I could say this for myself, if I hadn't taken advantage of the opportunities afforded to me and grounded myself in what was offered by the world and my family.

If someone looks at you and doesn't have the depth perception needed to understand the idea that your natural abilities were established through development over time and by sacrifice, this is not your business. Your life is not a debate and it certainly is not your job to analyze and allow this lack of comradery to make you second guess what you are doing or what could be possible. In fact, it's best if you lead by example and exude your light by being a model of exuberant self-love and focus. That is the key to forgiving others and looking past unfair treatment. Become so busy with who you are, concentrate on the concerns you have for yourself, and build up the resources and connections to turn your key in the door. If you do not, no one will. They can't see your door, only you can. You won't have time to wonder about where and why others are lacking, and this focus on them can lead you to leaving your door knob unturned with the key left in the keyhole. This stagnation and neglect of yourself is what leads to bitterness and resentment.

When I was just 15 years old I produced my first sold out concert. I booked Dorothy Norwood from the famous group called The Caravans. The original group members were Reverend James Cleveland, Shirley Caesar, Inez Andrews, Dolores Washington, Albertina Walker, Cassietta George, and Dorothy Norwood herself. When the group dispersed, each member reached individual super star levels.

After they all broke up, I got Dorothy Norwood to come from Atlanta, Georgia, to St. Paul's Community Baptist Church in Brooklyn. At that time the Reverend there was Adolofus S. Smith. The tickets were $3 to $5 dollars each and I paid her $500 dollars. When she first heard my voice over the phone and how young I sounded, she asked if she could please speak to my parents or someone else in charge.

"How'd you learn all this?" She wanted to know after I told her the program for the show.

"I'm the program chairman. I'm in charge of all the programs for the young people's choir—I know what you need. Just send me your contract, and I'll send you your deposit."

Her people were telling her, "I don't want you trusting this boy with this money!"

For the rest of her required fee, the choir raised the money by having chicken sandwich dinners.

The night of the concert, the church was packed. There wasn't any room left over for anyone else who showed up at the door. It was so successful. I had another concert fairly soon after that one. This time I had "The Hitmakers:" The Institutional Radio Choir, The Children's Choir of Institutional Church, and The St. Mark's Gospel Ensemble. That church was so packed that the police or the fire department came, and the church made so much money that I started my own company.

I started doing my own concerts independently at renowned venues such as New York University, Brooklyn College, Walt Whitman Auditorium, Brooklyn Academy of Music, the world renowned Apollo Theater, Manhattan Center, New York Tech, Friendship Baptist Church on Herkimer Street, Lincoln Center, and I can't leave out Madison Square Garden six times.

Life has always been a struggle for those that did not get fed with a gold spoon. When cigarettes were 25 cents, life was a struggle, and now they're 15 dollars, and it's still a struggle; when I had one of the first cell phones, life was a struggle. Live by knowledge and not faith. I know I can make it, because I've made it before, and I can make it now. I know I can make it, because I'm made for it.

Sometimes my floating offends other people, but is that going to stop me from flowing with the tides of my life? In the words of Maya Angelou, 'Does my sassiness offend you? Does my strut offend you?. . . I walk like I have oil wells pumping in my living room.' Go read the poem 'Ego Trippin' by Nikki Giovanni: 'I am so perfect, so divine, so ethereal so surreal, I cannot be comprehended except by my permission, I mean—I—can flyyyy; like a bird in the sky...'
People will look at you from the surface, and it's important not to alter yourself based on shallow perception. Don't you go altering how you sing, how you talk, and change who you are. Don't be offensive. Just balance.

From this chapter, I want you to gain the understanding that you need to have a clean heart. A clean heart opens your tongue and gives it power. A clean heart is assurance that you can do all the things you wish to do. Know that you cannot hate someone and expect love to come your way. Free yourself and allow your powers to move forward. So many times we go so far, and we go through so many things only to get to the answer right there inside of us. Always know that you are in a position of authority. Understand that authority comes from within just as our tongues stay fastened inside our mouths. The tongue is sharper than a two edged sword. Yet when we speak truth with love it is soothing and can heal a broken heart.

In conclusion, I want you to know that you need to free yourself from any feelings of confusion, aggression, revenge, or doubt. This way you will begin to reach a higher level. You will be able to see greater visions of true victory in your life. Your personal relationships will begin to move upward and forward. You'll be able to see a greater time at your job with your supervisor and colleagues. It's time for you to have the increase. Let it come forth with the love that you have inside of yourself.

CHAPTER 9
THE OTHER SIDE OF THROUGH

What do you do when facing those insuperable tragedies in your life? When darkness is the only light you can draw from...

Your business is gone, and your bank account is depleted. Your child has gone down the wrong path. Your marriage has sunk and not even a thread is holding it together. Life can sometimes hit you with a hard ball and leave you feeling without any protection or preparation; nowhere to run and nowhere to hide. Yet you've prayed and have gone to your synagogue, church, mosque, and countless other houses of worship. Still, life is blacker than a hundred midnights and with no hope in sight—where do you go from here? Is there a ray of restoration on the horizon? Is there a 'Somewhere over the Rainbow?' Truly speaking, is there even a rainbow? A silver lining?

Always remember wherever you are—there you are.

There's a place in each of you that can't be touched, tarnished, or tainted. Regardless of your hurdles, it can't be reached by anyone other than you. It's available to you in those quiet times. It's wherever you literally and figuratively are. It's there.

Firstly, pull yourself away from everything and anything other than you. Be assured that the "U" holds the remedies. As the "U" is used, it replenishes itself. Every time you call it forth, it's better and more reliable than a genie—you won't only get three wishes. Your

"U" is better and stronger than Samson even—his might was gone when his hair was cut. Your "U" is unlimited and replenishes.

Now stand still. . . When you feel like all is gone, and life seems hopeless without it, slow down and stop moving. Stand firm in your conviction.

Know that you have the power inside of you to move mountains: mountains of confusion, mountains of humongous setbacks, mountains of ill repute, and dissolved, faded relationships with family, friends and jobs. Mountains of financial destitution will be triumphed over as well.

PLEASE know—mountains can be moved. I know because I had towering mountains in my life. I'm a MOUNTAIN MOVER. They're all gone!!! Yes, gone. I've seen my mountains move. I was in the midst of the storm. Lightning was flashing, thunder was roaring, froth tipped sea billows were crashing, but I'm still here; not as a victim but as a victor. For victory is mine—join me today as we have walked through the fire.

Now it's time to shine like the diamond you are.

It's all found in your quiet times. During those quiet moments, start looking and preparing yourself for the other side of the tunnel. Paint the picture and make it clear. Allow that soft voice to speak to you. Listen, shhhhhh! Listen. So often we talk, cry, and yell our brains out. When all that is done, you find yourself in the same place with a sore throat. It's time now to open your eyes and look through the tunnel and see that what you have heard during your quiet times is now seeking you.

As you find solace and contentment with your newness of life be sure to share love. The love you share will keep the rivers of joy flowing. A few years ago, I received a request for help from a guy through one of my social media accounts. I did not know him, but we all know someone like him. Apparently he cheated on his wife, and she said enough is enough. He realized his mistake twice. Once when blindly executing the beginning of his demise. And again, finally, when the curtains at his show opened, and the closing of his show was at hand. These were my words to a stranger: Take time to look within yourself. Write a journal starting with 10-15 good qualities you have. You still have some! As the days go by, continue to expound on each of them. Take your time with this just as you took your time tasting the forbidden fruit that was not yours.

Now, write 15 things in your life that you must change and expound on each of them equally. Remember, "To thyself be true." Truth hurts, but it also heals. Sometimes, one needs to strip the paint totally off and then put a fresh coat of paint on. The new and improved you is more appealing than the shame and guilt that you have been wearing. The luster of your acceptance and forgiveness of self is pronounced with a better touch—a touch of class. That's the beginning of *The New You*.

Please do all this alone while not dealing with anyone about anything you've done. This work must be focused on what you're doing now in the present moment to and for yourself. "The New Man" is being sculpted slowly, perfectly designed, and ready for any obstacle in life.

After part one is completed and you've made peace with yourself. Call only those that you are strongly in need of and apologize for your wrong. Don't go deep; just short and from your new heart. Don't have any ulterior motive other than to release yourself from negative feelings of your past. Please know, it is not up to you if they choose not to accept your words. It's only up to you to honestly apologize. Don't deal with any hurt or pain from your girlfriend. She made her decision. . . just like you did. Don't carry any ill and don't try to win her back. That is the old you. Don't look for a pity party from anyone that will listen. Most importantly, don't speak negatively about her or the good times. If the person you hurt still wants to be with you, they will let it be known.

You can meditate without sitting with your legs folded and chanting. Doing daily meditations and 30 minute exercises, or at least walking alone will reconfigure your brain to focus on next steps while flushing out your system. If you're going to walk, try to walk in a new direction—one that's not near your ex-wife or ex-friend. You are creating "The New You" so walk alone. When you walk through your pain, hold your head up high. Don't fear your transformation. Just be confident and know the discomfort of healing yourself from your past mistakes is only ephemeral, it won't last.

At the end of a storm, there's a golden ray of hope which brings the melodious sounds that only nature can achieve. Can you begin to hear chimes ringing, voices singing, and birds chirping? So walk on through the hard times. . . Walk on through the misery of defeat.

Yes, your hopes and inspiration have been hit like a ping pong ball from side to side. Just walk into the newness of You. If you should decide to call your ex, YOU will know when to call (not to get her back) but just to say, "The old me is calling to say that the NEW me has taken over. I'm so very sorry for my actions, and I wish you all the best." Keep it short and honest. Don't try anything else. Let her know if she ever wants to just talk, you will be there with listening ears. If not, again, say I'm sorry and wish her the best.

I hope this gives you another way to view your plight. Another way to find solace which will give you some help.

Everyone makes errors.

CHAPTER 10
MY BACKGROUND IN MUSIC

When I was 6 I wanted a piano. I told my mother, and before I could think about what I really wanted there was a piano in the living room. I taught myself to play 'Peter Gunn' and 'I Found my Thrill on Blueberry Hill' by Fats Domino. She and my father were happy to hear me on the piano day and night. I was elated when I soon found out about my teacher, Maude B. Taylor, who was an outstanding, accomplished organist at the prestigious Cornerstone Baptist Church in Brooklyn, NY. There was only one slot available for lessons with Ms. Taylor, and this was on Saturday mornings at 7:30 a.m. The first two lessons were fun. Immediately after those initial lessons, I did not want to play any longer. I told my mother, but she wouldn't let me quit. I told my mother that Ms. Taylor would hit my fingers each time I made an error. Nevertheless, it did not matter, because I was stuck with her. I never practiced when I first started playing. I did not want to play at all. For those of you who knew my mother, you know I had no choice. . .

Fast forward to when I was about 12 years old, my mother received a call one Saturday at around 9:30 a.m. from David King Funeral Home in East New York, Brooklyn. The director explained to my mother that his pianist could not come in, and he would pay me $15.00 to play for under an hour. I did. After the funeral, he asked if I would like to play for another funeral at one o'clock for another $15.00. I said yes and, of course, he called my mother to get her consent and she agreed.

After the second service was over, I took the B14 Pitkin Avenue bus home for 15 cents. When I got off the bus at Pitkin and Hopkinson Avenue, I purchased a slice of pizza for another 15 cents. When I came home I had $29.70, and I felt like I had made it. Needless to say, I began practicing, and soon I was playing every Saturday for two and sometimes three funerals a weekend. I was 12 years old making $30.00 to $45.00 a week. Very soon thereafter, I was making $50.00 for each service I performed at. In the words of Aretha Franklin, "Need I say more…"

As I studied and my skill set continued to burgeon, I began playing for churches for $150.00 per Sunday by the age of 15. By that time I had already done several piano recitals at beautiful venues such as churches and senior care centers all over the United States. My mother would take me around the country to The National Baptist Convention with her. I got to play and sing while at these mega events and in the grand ballrooms of many prestigious hotels. The talk was spreading around the country about Jessie's little boy, Bobby.

By the time I was 16 years old, I was traveling back and forth by plane to California, playing and singing, hanging with several singers and musicians, and making a few more dollars. Excellent. I soon started my own choir called, 'The Children of God.' Wow! Did we have a ball! So many great singers and musicians all in one group. I was honored, because many of them were talented enough individually to have their own group, yet they chose to sing with me! What a pleasure and privilege. After many awards and accolades, I decided to go to the studio and do my first project. It was so cool listening to my choir album being played on the radio. Now I was doing interviews with radio and television stations; we were the talk of the town. The music bug had bitten me.

Very early in my late teens, I was asked to come and teach the children at PS 284. From then in 1983, I went on to teach at Trey Whitfield School, Boys and Girls High School, and Junior Academy.

While teaching, I had cameo spots on Sesame Street with Billy Taylor. I was also vocal coaching for one of Carlos Santana's singers. Each next step materialized as easily as the days of the week came around. I was even commissioned to assist Aretha Franklin for her show at Radio City Music Hall. The doors just flew open for me through the years of being involved in the industry. The consistent upward spiral was attributed to the synergism of how I never stopped honing my craft and how I always honored my talents by letting them lead me. I never really took that deep dive all the way into the secular music world, but my passion and skill made it more than conspicuous that I was doing exactly what I should be doing exactly when I should have been doing it.

I was now a very sought after musician. The answer within will nag at you to put in your time and do your work. The sign you're on the right track is when you feel concerned that you are not doing enough and your critical self is telling you that you better get it into gear soon or else! Never fear as the inspiration will seemingly be everywhere, including opportunities that at first start out small but as time goes by end up having you standing in awe at where your power has taken you. You are never late for your internal calling.

I successfully produced a host of major concerts including the McDonald's Gospel Fest at Madison Square Garden—a four-time sold out event—and the American tour for Joy Bell's Choir from Sweden; all the while remaining a passionate administrator, instructor, and motivator capable of inspiring diverse audiences.

The list eventually got longer and longer of artists that I produced in concert including:
Grammy Award Winning Artists: Al Green and Shirley Caesar at Brooklyn Academy of Music headed by my aunt, Elizabeth Lewis, Donnie McClurkin, Take 6, Yolanda Adams, Kirk Franklin, Hezekiah Walker, Tramaine Hawkins, Richard Smallwood, Vickie Winans, and Peabo Bryson.

Stellar Award Winning Artists: Karen Clark Sheard, Milton Brunson & Thompson Community Singers, Vanessa Bell Armstrong, Ricky Dillard, Mississippi Mass Choir, The Williams Brothers, The Georgia Mass Choir, Timothy Wright, Daryl Coley, Angie & Debbie Winans, Jonathan Slocumb, and Virtue.

I also made some television appearances and performances such as on Law and Order, Good Day New York (Fox TV), Good Morning America (ABC TV), The Today Show (NBC TV), and The Early Show (CBS TV). I co-hosted and produced McDonald's Gospel Fest, "Stand Up and Shout!" Special (ABC TV), I performed and sang on Sesame Street (PBS TV) and Hosted the Bobby Banks Show on WTHE Radio and WVIP Radio.

I produced more concerts at Madison Square Garden, The Apollo, Lincoln Center, Weills Recital Hall at Carnegie Hall, Cami Hall, Friendship Baptist Church. I had events at Walt Disney World three times and was producing at Green Pastures Church assisting Roger Hambrick. One of my most favorite, successful accomplishments with music has to be the McDonald's Gospel Fest. I was the producer for 4 years and volunteered for 12 years prior to being promoted.

I remember just as vividly as if it were yesterday, in the midst of me producing concerts all over the city, I still felt as though I wanted a higher purpose in life. I knew in my heart that I wanted to help more artists who were unknown and who did not have any sort of platform to begin performing at even a local level. I would sit and contemplate in my office as to what more I could do. I knew from an early age I would have a long, healthy, prosperous life without a doubt, but I worked as if this day was all I had, and I always welcomed having more on my plate. I knew from the words of Dr. Clarence Norman, "Keep goals in front of you," that keeping busy helps keep you whole. If you want to live a long time, make a long time goal and create incremental goals to fill your weeks and months. Very soon after I started having these thoughts and wishing for more, I received the call from Leslie Burnes. . .

After producing so many successful sellout shows, my name was well known and respected. McDonald's Gospel Fest was having several preliminary events throughout the New York tri-state area, and I was approached to become one of the judges. It was 1984 when I was asked to be a judge in the McDonald's Gospel Fest lineup by Leslie Burnes. She told me she was the producer for MGF and asked if I could help her by being a volunteer judge for the next set of preceding events. She already knew of my accomplishments and how she wanted to utilize that energy with upcoming gospel artists. I knew not who she was, but she knew me.

I knew nothing about McDonald's Gospel Fest, but I looked forward to it, because my focus was not money but on allowing my expertise to be the underlying factor of success for other people who aspired to develop their music careers. It was to be a metropolitan, statewide competition of singers, ensembles, choirs, and quartets. I had been given the gift at a young age as being a never ending source of everything I needed. All of my accomplishments came relatively easily to me, so to speak. I knew I was meant to give back, and this was the perfect pathway for me to do so. The hosted events would consist of local upcoming acts and artists from Connecticut, New Jersey, and all of New York.

My experience made me a great judge. I was well rounded with lots of information that came to me by way of traveling, playing, singing, and working with hundreds of talented acts and artists. Prior to my volunteer work with McDonald's Gospel Fest, I was the first promotor to bring in acts like Take 6 and Kirk Franklin who would each go on to win numerous Grammys. I had done booking at noteworthy theaters: The Brooklyn Academy of Music, Washington Temple, Charity Baptist, and Lehman Community College to name more. Leslie needed some stardom in the McDonald's line up, and she reached out to me because my track record was full of supreme talent and fresh faces.

We got started with a great lineup of twelve judges who I had curated. I realized soon enough that when I ask people to do something for me the norm is a 'yes' response due to the faith that others have in my integrity. Sometime around the beginning of spring, for 8 consecutive Saturdays, we would travel to meet at neighboring churches, schools, and venues throughout the area to listen to an array of musicians and singers. Sometimes two to three events were held per day. These events could start as early as 9 a.m., the next one would be at 2 p.m., and then another at 7 p.m. in different but proximal locations. Each event lasted between 3-4 hours. Sometimes they would overlap one another, and I would send a crew of judges to the other events while one was still going on. It all ended with our final event in the beginning of summer. Many politicians, public figures, preachers, and an array of congregates from many churches would attend our packed out shows.

Soon the festival had grown to even more local churches with thousands of more acts. I supplied the team with so many prominent figures within the industry to make up their cast of judges. Each of these judges had the same recognition if not more than I had in the industry. They were all powerful in their own rights. These high profile individuals had other jobs they had to fulfill, so they donated their time out of the love they had for helping young artists develop and hone their skills. From the beginning, I was looking toward the bigger picture. I was looking at what I could contribute to take this little festival being held in local churches, small event halls, and schools and turn it into something far more grandiose, because that is what the talent and everyone involved truly deserved and required. Soon the growth of the concerts and word of McDonald's Gospel Fest was spreading like wildfire. We had the best of the best on the judge panel including Mary Sharp, Stan Turner, Linda Brockington, Jerry Williams, Brother Paris, and many others.

Giving my best at every preliminary event at one point caused the head owner operator to take notice of how fast I was handing in my score sheet. It only takes me about 20-30 seconds to know if you can sing or not. We were given five minutes to score. I was told that because of my expertise in music, pitch uniform, choreography, and stage presence, it seemed as though I was quite possibly intimidating the contestants. I had to speak to the judges to make sure we were always on our P's and Q's. They had to know that many people were looking at us while we were looking and listening to the participants. We would go from venue to venue over the process of about two months to select the best of the best, and finally they would then have a final competition at the main venue which would be at a local church or school in each state. Political people would come in and give proclamations, citations, and awards. We would have all local artists headline the finals or main events at that time. This went on for approximately nine to ten years.

This became more of a job than I had expected. Being the head judge meant that I had to make sure that all the artists who appeared at the preliminary events were ready to go on time and that they had the knowledge of all the rules and regulations. I inherently became the senior judge, because all of my colleagues and all of the owners and operators saw me as such since I was the one reaching out to all of my respective friends in the industry to join anytime someone on the team was pulled back to their duties and main projects. Everyone I asked always said yes. Many would come during the next ten years and many would leave, yet there were a few key people who stayed for the long haul.

The work was arduous at best. Yet I insisted everyone on my team remember the brand name, McDonald's, which was done in excellence at all times. This great team and I changed the direction of McDonald's Gospel Fest. The Jenkins Brothers were the hosts and they were absolutely the greatest tag team match I've ever seen. Between the jokes, stories, introductions, singing duets, and their spiritual overtones, they certainly crowned the exuberant festival every year.

Ron Bailey, who was one of the main owners in the McDonald's restaurant chain with over twenty McDonald's restaurants in the area, and the other restaurant owner-operators were all satisfied with what I was doing. They noticed how I was leading with dignity, finesse, and a professional attitude that represented myself and McDonald's. I never knew I was looked up to by them. I found that out much later; however, it would not have mattered. I am a strong advocate of acting the way you want to be and soon you'll be the way you act.

Leslie, who asked for my assistance, had a major falling out with the powers that be, and I witnessed their argument in 1995. The only thing I could do was say, 'Unfold baby, unfold." I knew then that the end result would be my journey into my next step of the answer within. Two weeks later, I received a phone call from Ron Bailey, and he asked me if I would consider heading Mcdonald's Gospel Fest and taking over the production of it. I knew this call was coming twelve years ago when I received the invitation for judging. I said that I would be willing to sit down and have a talk. I got myself prepared for the meeting which was about a week later. Sometimes you just know certain events are going to happen, but you might not know how they will exactly transpire to bring you into your reality.

Soon I was no longer a judge, I was the producer of what I had envisioned inside of myself. We picked up our finalists and went all over to different churches and heard different choirs to pick out some of the best acts. When I reviewed what they needed me to do, I wanted it to be fair and above reproach. McDonald's name was known everywhere you go. It stood for good fast food and a clean environment where everyone could feel welcome including people of all ages, nationalities, and creeds. Great musicians, directors, and singers would help me to sign off on this job. I did not have to look far in order to find the major east coast players in the industry.

I remember one time Les Brown said he was going to get this radio show position. He had always visualized himself as a disc jockey. One day he went to the radio station he worked for, and the guy doing the show was drinking so heavily he could not conduct himself. Les wanted his job and realized that this guy's journey toward his answer within was going to be that he was going to ruin his position at his radio show before he was going to eventually clean up his act. Les said this was going to be his opportunity. Sure enough one night the DJ was so wasted, Les got the call from the boss. He asked Les if he could go into the DJ booth, because the DJ's speech was so impaired, and take over the controls. He wanted Les to 'babysit' the live show until he could get someone in there to cover him. Les got on the radio and the rest was history—"Look out this is me, L B triple B, Les Brown your platinum playing poppa—there were none before me, and there will be none after me—therefore, that makes me the one and the only. Young and single and love to mingle. Indubitably qualified to bring you satisfaction, a whole lotta action. Look out baby, I'm your love man," he said on-air to listeners. When retelling this story to 80,000 people at the Georgia Dome in 1993, he makes the connection that, "When you're hungry, you'll put anything in your mouth to eat." In addition, "If you want something bad enough," Les says, "and all your dreams and schemes are about it, with the help of God and with the strength of God, you will achieve your dreams." That's how I knew Ms. Burnes didn't have long because she was struggling, and I knew that I could add much more to the production. The position was right for me as someone who had already worked to transform the festival so much from only a seemingly small volunteer role.

When things happen for you it may seem like an uncontrollable whirlwind. You may feel as if the world is tipping over, and you're about to fall completely into the unknown. Don't be anxious. Sometimes blessings in life work out only when a bit of chaos ensues, shaking things up a bit for them to be reordered the way they most need to be. If something is not for you, it won't be for you. This is why you can sit back and relax, because if you know you're the one for the job or for the task, it's coming no matter how it looks at a given moment.

When Leslie had her falling out with the board, I didn't immediately know what was going to happen next. All I knew then was that I had to stand by my laurels and could not be a part of the gossip or the quarrel and tarnish my name and reputation. Even though there were only a few people who saw the argument they had behind the church, it just seemed like everyone in our community was going to find out how much of a disorganized mess we were responsible for. Ron and several other owner operators witnessed the whole ordeal along with some of my judges and a few participants. Of course I had my ideas and notions, but I also felt as though there were other places for me. In the middle of all the drama, I grounded myself in the fact that this festival and how far we had come was not just something I could walk away from. I also didn't want the situation to ruin the reputation of what Leslie had done. She was a strong-willed woman, and she was extremely talented with the execution of these events. Focusing on the inside allowed me to know to stand still and see the salvation of the lord. She would end up moving on, and I had a strong enough inkling that I would pour over these problems and heal something that wasn't necessarily broken, just a little bit hurt.

Obviously, my phone was ringing off the hook about this malay that took place in the rear of the church yard between Leslie and the executives. The judges, participants, and even guests heard Ms. Burnes giving her colleagues a piece of her mind and it was quite a sight to say the least. Surprisingly, it never made the news but word-of-mouth sometimes could be worse. I always monitored what I said on the phone or face-to-face with people. There are instances when people try to sabotage you by saying what you said to them or twisting your words to fit their projections of life. No one has permission to affect your life by their idea of who you are, so don't give them any reasons to think they're right in doing so. Your garden is beautiful and needs your full focus and attention; for what you grow are the only crops you may eat. The nursery rhyme says, 'Be careful little tongue what you say.'

Pretty soon I received that phone call from Mr. Bailey which gave Gospel Fest a new beginning and myself a new attitude. Wow! After his long prelude and small talk, I was asked to come to the Ronald McDonald House on the East Side of Manhattan. After the call ended, I began singing, "Well, we're moving on up to the Eastside, to that deluxe apartment in the sky." They had a position open for me as the producer for McDonald Gospel Fest. I wanted to take it out of the churches and do our main event at Madison Square Garden. Everyone would look at me like I was insane, but I was serious. I knew what was missing. What I brought to the table is what I wanted to do and there would be no stifling it.

Going into that initial meeting, I knew I had to be organized and impressive. I wanted to talk about my views on taking it to the next level with class and sincerity. I let him know that I was going to be accepting his invitation confidently and that I was looking forward to meeting him the following week. School was still in session, I shared absolutely nothing with the people around me. I called out of school that day, got dressed in a sharp looking suit, took the Long Island Railroad to Manhattan, and then a cab to east 73rd street.

The weather outside was beautiful, the wind was gentle, and the air was comforting to the touch. The sound of cabs and traffic all of a sudden took on a whole new meaning. I had grown up and spent my whole life in this wonderful city, and now I felt like my services were taking on a befitting role created just for me. As I entered the corporate room, they invited me to sit at the head of the table. There were 15 or 20 people there who I didn't know very well from the last twelve years of volunteering as a judge and even some people I had never met before.

The board began to talk to me about their vision. They began to tell me about all the things that I had done over the last twelve years and how meaningful my contributions were. They also reminded me of something that I did in Upper Room Church in Dix Hills,

Long Island. I wrote and taught a song on the spot there. I had all the participants singing together. The judges were astonished. I did this in front of 4000 people and about 2000 of them were participants. They were flabbergasted at how I wrote and taught a song to everyone. This event began with me being at the microphone saying, "Hello, how are you doing? I'm Bobby Banks and you are the next participants of McDonald's Gospel Fest." In my bravado, I continued, "I want to have a quick quiz, and I've got a gift for you! Who can name all of the singers of The Caravans? And when you speak you have to name them all or else you can't win." Someone attempted to name them, but they missed a couple members. "Almost but not quite!" Another contestant came up and mismatched names. "So close!" Finally someone won, and I told them to come up to the stage.

I gave them coupons to use at McDonald's Restaurant for their whole family and everybody clapped and celebrated. "Before we start this competition," I began my proposition. "Let's do something as one, as a whole, and bring out the best we have to glorify God and seal the glory of His fellowship." I started tickling the piano and about a minute and half later, I spoke. "Okay, I got a little hook here." I addressed all of the vocal ranges, instructing the sopranos to sing a part, all the tenors, and all the altos. In that space we came up with lyrics together to go with my hook, and everyone sang different parts. We harmonized and created what someone might call a miracle. The owner operators who were there were awestruck. That's how we started the competition that day. It pays to be authentic and true to yourself. You never know who is watching and discerning. However, you must always operate in excellence because that's your name, that's your legacy, and that's what you will be remembered by. I always practice the saying that you are no better than your last time doing something.

They loved my choices of judges and how my operations worked so smoothly. Sitting, eating and talking for over three hours I closed by saying to them, "I am honored to have been asked for this position, however, in order to do what I am envisioning for this great company and the great people that we serve, I know that McDonald's Gospel Fest is meant to have a far greater reach. Let's transition the main event out of the local churches and take it to Madison Square Garden." That—right there—caused everybody's eyes to pop open like, 'Boy has lost his mind!' I knew everyone at the table had power, money, and a big title in the corporation. . . However, I had the idea and the know-how. I said to the heads, "If each of us do what we know we can do, this event would propel our production to a level as big as your Happy Meal! That's what you hired me for after all," I told them. So in the words of Mary, Mary, 'take the chains off your feet and let's dance!'

We went back-and-forth, chewing on that for another 20 minutes, but I would not budge. I knew myself too well. I knew who I was and where I was headed. Personally, I was headed to Madison Square Garden—if McDonald's was with me, they were going too. They couldn't hear what I heard, and they couldn't see what I saw. I had a pulsating force within me that was about to burst right open. Now I can almost comprehend an aspect of a woman's experience when she is birthing a child. It's there, it's in there, and now it's got to come out. I respect every woman and every mother for bringing knuckle heads like me into the world.

The executives were worried about money, but I had been so deep in the trenches that it was obvious to me that the event was going to be a success. The exact equation to make this thing what it needed to be was that the gospel festival had to be at a level of the entire McDonald's corporation. This corporation had so many locations outside of the country, and in the U.S. they were everywhere. It's McDonald's—going big or going home was a no brainer.

I said to the executives that it's not important how much money you make for tickets. "The most important thing, ladies and gentlemen, is to brand your name at Madison Square Garden." Can you imagine the world's most famous arena and the world's most famous fast food restaurant coupling together via Bobby Banks? It costs smiles, laughter, and brings back your total budget and then some.

After getting back home, there was only one person that I needed to speak to and that was the genius herself, Pat Biassi. She and I worked at the same school. She was a science teacher, and I was a music teacher. Funny also, she lived diagonally across the street from me on the same block. She is no joke—plus she is as smart as a whip and as classy as anyone can be. The best part was we knew each other for many years by way of her precious mother, Marguerite McCunneyhead. Mrs. McCunnyhead was the president of the Willing Workers, a church fundraising and volunteer group, and she and Deacon Oscar Johnson Sr. nourished me in my early years playing in church. I could really trust her and her daughter. I met her daughter Pat through the same church, Bethlehem Baptist, even before I started teaching music at their school which was Bethlehem Baptist Academy. Pat would come to visit her mother who worked as a cook in the church cafeteria. She would come see her mom and watch me play music during each church service. I loved Pat and her mother. They were both beautiful and intelligent women.

You never know how one person can lead you to another. It behooves us all to monitor how we respect and treat each other on this journey called life. All I had to do was just have Pat on it all. We would talk on the phone or in my office and work everything out. We would talk and after we finished she would forward me spreadsheets with bullet points and all the information concisely summarized making me look like the president of the corporation. Since it was now time for my second meeting with the powers that be, that following week Pat Biassi and I went to Manhattan to see what was up. Obviously, I had Pat with me all the way there. Prior to this big meeting, she had done all of her work assisting me pro bono because we were such good friends. After the meeting, I was able to hire her.

Sometimes you just know when someone is going to be your friend. When I heard Pat's vocabulary, I knew we would get along. She was like me and someone I knew who I could have a deep, authentic bond with. She came with me the following week to the headquarters on the Upper East Side. We went up to the corporate room located above the floors dedicated to McDonald's philanthropic mission of providing room and board to parents and their children. Their corporate floor had grand mahogany tables that could hold about twenty-five people with large luxurious leather chairs and all kinds of cameras and video equipment for presentation.

When we went in, Pat gave me the folders and binders to hand out to everybody. Everything was printed with my name on it. All of my accomplishments and events were included in the presentation. My quest for bringing the gospel side of McDonald's to light, while tying in the community, was clearly mapped out and organized in the plans. They didn't know me before this; they knew of my work as a senior judge but not the business side of me.

When we finished with my presentation, their mouths were dropped open, and their pens were out to sign. They were excited to move forward with the new ideas and their new producer. In short, I was offered the job to head the entire McDonld's Gospel Fest. With joy, I immediately started to work on the next year's event.

After I got the position, I was representing the brand name. I was on cloud nine, because I knew deeply that I was destined for this project. The confidence you feel when you know nobody can do a project the way you can because you offer too much and bring too much internally is elating. I knew it was going to happen BIG. I wanted it and I got it. My first year was right on the money—Madison Square Garden. McDonald's Gospel Fest caught so much media attention. It felt like the whole city was promoting what I was doing. I had more artists on the show than anyone could possibly have had, because I knew what to do. All of my years in the game, and all of my producing and promoting, made me entirely tapped into the exact circuits needed to put what I was a part of on the map. Months later after the final meeting, the day of the concert was now at hand. The crowd was ushered in, and it was my first time at The Garden as a producer. . . SOLD OUT!

It absolutely blew my mind to see my name in lights on the front marquee of The Garden. I remember standing outside the day before with tears in my eyes as my name would appear every 3 minutes: Produced by Bobby Banks.

Over the next four years, McDonald's Gospel Fest was held at Madison Square Garden and produced by yours truly, Bobby Banks. Each main event was anticipated by enthusiastic waiting audiences. It was a star-studded extravaganza every year with such luminaries as Orland Draper, Richard Smallwood, Hezekiah Walker, Kim Burrell, Tremaine Hawkins, John P. Kee, obviously Timothy Wright, Vickie Winans, and many others. Timothy Wright was one of my favorite artists to book because he was an all around great musician and performer.

That initial, foundational Madison Square Garden event involved a lot of planning. You don't realize how much really goes into events of this size and caliber. Besides booking artists, hiring the sound company, obtaining backline equipment, acquiring limousine companies, you also have to organize airfare and schedules for performers and technicians. Their hotels must be secured and all of the craft, which is the catering for the artists in the green room before and during the event, must be up to par. A whole team is in charge of producing fliers and posters. Radio and TV commercials are to be created and paid for, along with other advertising for the weeks and months leading up to the big day. When insurance and legal have all they need from you, you still must make sure you have the right artists and that they are all satisfied with everything that is panning out. The right artists will promote the show with just their name alone. The live show's flow depends on the script writer, assistant promoters, the precise allocations for dressing rooms, stage managers, photographers, interviewers, and runners. All of this was just the beginning, however, I had no problem. . . My mother prepared me for this when I traveled with her around the country producing her plays, "The Creation," "Mary's Baby," and many others.

By this time I had my backbone, Will Bogle. He was really my missing link. His integrity, skillful approach, and leadership were never superfluous or unappreciated. The effects of his nature and alignment with me made for many more years of prosperity and wellness to come. Please do not take for granted the people in your life who tell it like it is and speak to you straight. Maybe you even relate to Will. I know I do. I could give him an assignment and it was almost always done better than what I had intended or asked him for. Bogle is one of the best in the industry, not to mention he is as smart as they come. He handled my TV special as if it were his own. He operates in excellence and does not need to apologize for it. Even this week he was challenging me to grow more and do more. He delights in others doing well.

It pays to treat people like a cigarette lighter and not a match. If you use people without any intention of continuing onward with them, you never get to see their brilliance or exuberance work in your life while they simultaneously live theirs, ever again.

The four year job was joy unmeasurable and work unbelievable, yet the result was 4 sold out, spectacular events. My last show was the 4th show and it was taped and televised. The television special on ABC was called "Stand Up and Shout! McDonald's Gospel Fest."

Prior to this last show, I thought it would be best to approach the owner operators to say it's time for TV. By now my stocks had gone up. There were no longer jaws dropping and mouths left open after I spoke. There was only anticipation each time I walked into the boardroom. My successful track record allowed me to have the freedom to express those things that were within to bring them to the surface.

I had the esteemed pleasure of meeting and working with the legend himself, Art Moore from ABC. He and I worked together to bring this TV special to a multiplicity of homes. The name "Stand Up and Shout: McDonald's Gospel Fest" was unanimously accepted and ran with.

Everywhere I looked preceding the event, there were cameras recording everyone. They were at my Long Island home so much until I thought I needed to receive them as members of my family. So many hours of pre-recording goes into a show of this magnitude. The cameramen and women traveled for weeks to churches and rehearsals; they taped interviews, and they recorded us during downtime and playtime as well.

I knew that the 4th sold out show at Madison Square Garden was going to be a live televised taping before it was even spoken about. It was also going to be a culmination of all that I had done. When I went forward and spoke with Art and his team, they gave me full support for producing my first TV special. Everywhere I went with the cameras recording me, recording the artists, going to our homes, watching us eat, looking at us playing, and going with us to rehearsals made me feel like I was walking around in my own dream.

Yes. You can do this. Anything you see for yourself, you can have. I am no different, no better, and no more smart than you are; however, I do know if you reach deep down inside, the things that happen for you will be better than the things you think you want to happen to you. So in the words of Walter Hawkins, "Don't wait 'til the battle is over to shout; shout now, because you know at the end, you're gonna win."

The day of the event at Madison Square Garden, Art allowed me to 'do me.' Art Moore's team spent days and weeks cutting and splicing all of the footage from all of the activities that we had filmed for the show. The result was a huge success. One of my favorite memories was inviting 100 people to my home to sit down in my yard by the pool. We were outdoors, enclosed around 3 large TV screens, with food being served like crazy, and everybody watching and listening for the 8:58 p.m. commercial: "Next after this break, Stand Up and Shout McDonald Gospel Fest."

Before the show started we all fell silent. A hush spread around the yard, and the show began while tears streamed down my face. I realized at that moment the answer within had come at the exact right time.

All four sold out shows were humongous and star studded events. Even with Will by my side, there was something missing. I must pay respect to Alecia Mason. She is a professional in all that she is and does. What a support in production she was, I can't even begin to tell you. Alecia and I went to the same church for years, and I never knew she was responsible for Lou Rawl's Parade of Stars. What a match for McDonald's Gospel Fest! Sometimes the thing or person you need to help with a task is right next to you and you don't see it until it's time. Our friendship and close proximity were destined for our mutual success. She was and is gentle, yet extremely knowledgeable. It pays off being around others who know how to get things done. Alecia was well versed in the technical side of the industry including how all of the equipment worked. She was very instrumental in helping me and making sure that Gospel Fest was done in splendor and grandeur. She had skills that I didn't have like working the teleprinter, so you can have control of what's being said on the stage. She also had knowledge of 'globals,' an industry phrase for the colorful lighting that shines down on the stage, which are ordered in different color schemes that change as the artists perform. Will and Alecia were both working together at different ends of the production spectrum. They never bumped heads and the dynamic was always positive. They were both in their strengths. While Alecia took care of the technical side of things, Will was meeting and greeting artists, making sure their dressing rooms were set up just right for them. Both of them ensured that Bobby Banks Production and Management was well respected and had a strong reputation of professionalism and success; they also both kept me in check.

Too often we can get stuck in a rut and feel like we are pounding out hours of work unnoticed and for nothing, but our efforts never go unnoticed by ourselves and the love that guides us. You are always preparing yourself to be in alignment and to hear the answer within. If you are a good worker, stay present in mindset, even in fog-laden waters. Soon the obstructions to your sight will lift, and you will see that the work contributed was all worth it, because now you are around those that match your qualifications and experience with their own authentic and unique qualities. I could have never done what Alecia did on staff for McDonald's Gospel Fest. The same way I needed her, I also needed Will, and they both came to me at the right time and for the right reasons. The three of us, William, Alecia, and I, had our hands exponentially full with the tasks that seemed to be reserved just for us because of the answer we each had within us our whole lives leading up to those wonderful years. It was amazing to see them in the zone. I see now how my magnetic force of attraction was matched and developed. Working with my crew was like the song by the Ohio Brothers, "Fire." The synergism was next to none. We added to each other's cups until they ran over. Alecia wasn't afraid of me and I wasn't afraid of her, likewise, Alecia and Will never carried resentment toward one another, because all of our lives had boiled down to that very moment. Our show went off without a hitch.

When that final concert was behind me, I wanted to move forward in another arena. There is always someone sitting, looking, and observing your movements. I knew that this thing had capitulated and morphed into something bigger than my vision. With that, I knew that somewhere around me was my Judas. Not long thereafter, I was told Golden Harris, McDonald's PR firm, had hired a person of their choosing to produce the now star studded, four-time sell out event at Madison Square Garden. After Leslie had left 4 years prior, they had hired Carolyn Jones who took care of all things concerned with public relations. Everything involved with McDonald's and their publicity was her job to oversee. She was my direct contact for the 4 years I was hired to produce the festival. My relationship with Ms. Jones never reached the level of compatibility that I had with other members of the team, however we moved forward. After I produced the television show, she hired another producer of her choice. She passed away there after, and the next person they hired after that was Curtis Farrow, who is still making the magic happen. He has done and is still doing a phenomenal job.

I received a letter from Art Moore, who was the executive producer from ABC in charge of production on the show and who was also WABC-TV's vice president of programming. He was amazed at how well I produced my television special, 'Stand Up and Shout.' He wrote me a letter of recommendation upon my request, because I was looking to produce a big event the following year. I received a beautiful letter from Art, and I was able to forge forward—onward and upward.

The things that I had worked for were beginning to come to fruition, because the answer was manifesting itself into full display.

All of this happened, one day at a time. . . Until it was my day. I am a true believer. 'Don't wait till the battle is over to shout…' Start at 6 years old, 10, 17, 25, 50 or even 75 years of age and never give up. You will have some hurdles to jump over—and God said: "That's Good." Why? Because every hurdle, every 'no,' every fall down puts you closer to your time—closer to your: 'Yes.' In the words of my friend Les Brown, "If you can look up…You can get up."

I triumphed each year at Madison Square Garden producing and promoting sold out McDonald's Gospel Fest events during those unforgettable years. When I came before the board at last and told them I wanted to do a one hour TV special, they had already seen my answer come alive in their world just as much as it did in mine; because I never gave up and kept putting my best foot forward, the most important moments of my career came around. What was once called 'insanity' was by the end considered 'mastery' by members of the board.

My hands have been involved with many other aspects of life such as weddings, vacation planning, anniversary parties, cars, buses, churches, furs, teaching, motivational speaking, piano and voice lessons, and so on. However, my greatest love was fathering my children and being married to my loving wife, Elaina Joy Sanabria-Banks.

CHAPTER 11
IT'S STILL AMAZING

For years I've worked not knowing that these great things happening in my life were happening because of my own mindset. My perspectives triggered a connection to allow me to move through this world with splendor and grandeur.

I finally found out the power was within me when I began listening to motivational speakers. Their methodology worked really well and made sense to me. However, I was working their programs to the point where it didn't seem like I had ownership.

So many times we go so far and we go through so many things only to get to the answer right there inside of us. I know this book will give you the key to recognize that the answers are sometimes the closest things to reach for and the simplest solutions to think of. The answers are already in you. When you think about yourself, you'll get the answers so easily because it's like a spark of lightning. God gives us the power to make things happen. The answer will hit you and make you smile. Greater things shall you do. You think I'm the Mac Daddy? You're the Mac Daddy, because you have the power within you.

I look back, and I reflect on the greatness that has been engraved inside of me. I can feel it. It gives me joy and humility wrapped in one. The underlying factors of success are love, forgiveness, and perseverance.

The years 2018 and 2019 were life-changing and have greatly strengthened the powers that I possess. I knew that in order for this year to end the way I wanted, I could not allow any weapons to form against me. That negativity I avoided included malice, gossip and ill-feelings. I could write a book on just these past few years alone. I've seen how people can build their level of so-called "success" on the backs of people who genuinely mean well.

I remember one day at work, someone came running down the hall towards me. I thought they had lost their mind. They began to scream, point their fingers at me, huff and puff, and try to blow the building down.

I tried to deescalate the situation by asking, "May I speak to you, please?"

"No," was the reply. "Don't say a word."

It was then that I knew that a 'kick in the butt in the right direction' can be good for you—which was a quote from my daddy. I knew at that moment it was time for me to leave. This was when I had a teaching position at a school where I gave my life striving to help children from the area.

Immediately after this supervisor blew up on me in the hallway, she came into my room to do a formal observation. I was able to keep my calm demeanor and composure. I was no stranger to high stakes environments and having the pressure put on while I was performing, even if this time I was in front of small children. When I received my observation sheet, all of the categories had Cs and Ds. . . I don't even dress a 'C' or 'D'. . . Not even on my worst day am I a 'C' or 'D.'

When I went to her office, I had to ask her what my score was all about. I inquired about how there could be nothing, after my 50 years of being an instructor, that reached higher than a C or a

D in the areas being examined. In other words: How much more preparation should the 50 years of my teaching experience allow me to have? Or are you just saying you don't like me? I left.

Resigned.

When you sacrifice, when you have these positions that take so much of your person and the totality or who you are (respectfully because I don't want to be condescending about anyone or to make myself look good), you shouldn't accept less than what you deserve. If you provide honesty and integrity, that is what is required for you in return. This book has been a healing device for me. What about you, my new extended family? I want you to continue growing. We can't grow by making people feel bad. I have given many years of service to several churches, and I was not the type of person that needed to put others down in order for me to be up. This has never been my archetype, and I believe this is due to my focus and perseverance to be who I am to the fullest while acting on the answers within. Someone who needs to demean and insult others indicates that they're already low.

Sometimes it's hard to leave a place and know your worth. In the words of Billy Paul, 'When love is new…' Just like at a new job, you can see the connection between a first date. On a first date, guys would open the car door and wait until our date was seated. In the beginning at our new job, our supervisors are all smiles and giving us the thumbs up. When we were dating someone in the beginning of the relationship, sometimes we would call in the middle of a song on the radio and say, 'Turn to WBLS and listen to this song.' In the beginning of your first year at a workplace, everyone still wants to impress you. During the blossoming of your relationship, you would just call to say, 'Hey, just getting ready to go to the store…' You would buy a card just to buy a card. When love is new, just like when you move to a new job or a new work environment, everything is bliss. Sometimes it can be that all those niceties were illusions on display.

I don't need empty compliments. I'm satisfied with 'thank you.' I don't need accolades. I like smiles on people's faces. I like when the warmth of the harmony is so tantalizing, the rhythm is carried and moves to the words of a song, bringing the piece to another level; when the expression and dynamics under the melody sing. I like when that causes the sound to be electrified until the point when the music would take the lyrics to almost not being words but pure feeling—soulful vibrations. I work hard on my craft and how I can get it to flow from me to the choir, undoubtedly creating a sanctuary.

Once at a church I played for, the minister would always say something motivational to the choir after the service. His usual speech to us eventually started to turn negative and less encouraging and positive. Sundays would slip into months, and months slipped into years.

In order to keep you at a certain pace so you can't be too over praised by the people in charge, others will stop being authentic with you—if they ever were. They don't feel comfortable with the realization that you don't have a lid or a glass ceiling above you. If someone is beginning to speak condescendingly about your craft, let it empower you. After all, it only makes you realize 'middle c' is 'middle c' no matter where you go. It saddened me to leave, but the answer within took me where I had to go. I'm not even talking about how the salary was four times as much as before or how I was now working at a more prestigious venue; it was the peace that lifted me. With such a transition, it was less about the new perks of my job and more about my emotional health and wellbeing.

Sometimes the burden can get heavy and the road can get rough. James Cleveland said, "No cross, no crown." Sometimes we have to sit under a dark cloud and appreciate the silver lining. Get out your tears at night to get a cheer in the morning, and allow the sadness to get washed away. Do know, in the words of Timothy Wright, 'Trouble don't last always.' Joy does come in the morning.

One would ask, how could you find love for the person who is offending you? But, someone's offense enables me to open my eyes and realize that mediocrity is mediocrity no matter where you go. Today I am freer than I have ever been. "Free is free." If you're free, you're free, you don't have to worry about anything else. If you're successful, you're successful. If you're doing well in life, forget about the outside noise. You have to look at things for what they are and where they are coming from. It's what's inside of you that matters. What was put inside of you was not put there by man, so man can not take it away. In the words of Nikki Giovanni, "I can fly like a bird in the sky."

A lot of times, we might begin to look at the things around us, and we hear ourselves say that we were right all along. You don't need to be a viper and lash out after feeling stomped on. Stay in the lane of love and add to the powers only God can give you. Why block your victory with sabotage? Allow your victory to enable more victories. Allow your greatness to be not just meant for you but for others as well. Allow for an open flowing relationship between the source of power that you have and help to enable others to move forward and upward just like how you are. When this is done, every round and everyone goes higher and higher. 'Self' is a powerful thing. 'Self' will tell you that someone is mistreating you. 'Self' will say it's not right that you have to do this. 'Self' will say—listen to how you're being spoken to.

So, I had to do what I am recommending to my readers. I had to step outside of myself and look at the entire scenario. I wanted to make sure that I could rest my head on my pillow and not sweat the small stuff. Please be reminded of Warner Wolf on television who said, "Let's take it to the video." In those days, they didn't have advanced instant replay the way we have today; even still, they would show the replay of the incident in question. I had to do a replay on my life.

The camera is there in my mind. It's embedded there and it stands high above me. When I've completed any task that is of importance to me, I roll the video back in my head. I check it out to ensure that I have moved in the right direction. I'm talking about the kind of love where you don't accept less than you desire, even from yourself—most importantly, from yourself. I'm talking about deeply releasing your pain and anguish. If you don't, you will wind up carrying it. So, you choose, which one do you want to do? I'm advising that when the road is rough, the going gets tough, and the hills are sometimes hard to climb, but with strength and a powerful mindset you can master any given situation. As long as you can speak it and believe it, it is yours for the taking.

The destinations you wish to travel toward have to be envisioned by you. You have to get to know your intended goal and practice traveling to this location first in your mind. Know where you are going and call it from the inside. Once I see what I want, I lock my sights on it and it's done. I have the test of time on my side. I've already done it all, because I visualized the journey from the inside. Seeing it all get done using the answers I guided myself to is like recognition of familiar landmarks and road markers. What ends up happening on the outside has already been tested. I don't have to do anything but look inside. If you want to say I'm cheating, say I'm cheating; if you want to get in trouble, get in good trouble. I already have the answer. I already took the test. I have the answer key. I passed the exam, because the answer was inside of me. Cultivate it, feed it. The answer is within us, and you need to reintroduce yourself to the truth even though it already knows you better than you think you know yourself. Many times the answer came out favorably in my life and showed me that this way of thinking was enough for me to rely on. I've tried the answer within when it was not developed. The trial and error period led me to experience and over time it was fool proof. It's a muscle you have to practice in order to bat 1000. Loosen up what's inside of you and let your full spectrum come into play.

Now as each year gets ready to close, I no longer carry the bondage of attempted entrapment. My daughters and I have traveled everywhere in America. They have attended the best schools, crossed the Atlantic Ocean, including the Mediterranean Sea, and even the Nile River. Our best is yet to come. So, don't fear when you must leave. Never find yourself locked in a position that will cause your heart to bleed. Simply move forward.

Let's look back at a recent situation. I worked in an area which was highly populated. One result of this was scarce parking. One morning, I drove around for a few minutes, but I could not find a space that would appease me. I got so fed up, I pulled up next to the car that was in the spot I wanted. "Lady, would you come downstairs?" I called out in the car. "I know you are late for work!" Two minutes later, a woman came running outside and got into her car. She quickly moved out of my spot.

On a bigger scale, I began examining what I wanted as the culminating experience of the past year. I decided that I wanted to sell my home and move somewhere new. I decided to take my two girls, hit the road, and leave the Big Apple. The move from New York to my house in Jersey was necessary. I had come to realize the house in Long Island was not conducive to raising my family without my wife. I needed to be closer to my sister, Sharon.

We began looking for a place to rest our heads. We began to pack boxes and call movers and brokers. It was an exhilarating experience within itself. I had to prioritize what was important. Which is why I encourage you to write your vision. The most important thing was to find a blue ribbon school district. If I may reiterate, and I tell my daughters the same—the most important factor is to keep yourself anchored with an eyesight that will allow you to move forward. Make sure you have strong knowledge of English, math, traveling, and music. Those are the areas I feel we should all work on. I asked myself: where can I get the sum of these things? We wrote down our expectations. I wrote that I wanted to live on a tree-lined street. I needed a place where I could teach people to sing and play the piano. At the end of the list, I wrote that I wanted to get rid of one of my cars. The list got so long that the items seemed impossible. I knew I was ready for another victory. And everything came as I expected!

Now, those are the lists that I like! The ones where you look back and don't believe it can be possible, because if it was possible, we wouldn't have to work so hard to manifest. The day before the movers came, I had everything I wanted in a house, but I still had not gotten rid of my car. I placed ads in a few magazines, only to receive several goofy calls. I even posted about it on Facebook. People would message me saying how beautiful the car was, but no one wanted to buy her. On top of that, my daughters kept asking about the car. My response to them was, "It's sold!"

"It's sold?" they asked, confused. "But… We just went into the garage and it was still there."

"It's sold!" was my only reply to them.

I knew the car would get sold to someone sincere. My car was already off the market—I just didn't know who was buying it. The well kept Bentley was waiting for its new owner; someone specifically meant to drive her home. When I could not find anyone to make the purchase, I decided I was going to stop, relax, and move forward with cleaning the car like I was preparing it to be driven by her new owner.

Early during the morning of my move, I received a call from an old preacher friend of mine asking about the price of the car. He expressed interest. That was at 9:00 a.m. By 12:30 p.m. we were leaving the bank where he withdrew money to purchase the car. The car was sold!

That Saturday morning, while I was doing the prep work on the car, I didn't know how it was all going to work out. I had faith that it would, and I had forged ahead as if that were all part of a plan. "Daddy, what are you doing?" My daughter asked. I told her that someone was buying the car and I had to clean it. "Daddy, you are crazy," she remarked, shaking her head, knowing no one had responded to any of the ads. Not even 10 minutes later, that's when the phone rang. That's when the minister called asking what the deal was with the car I was selling. I told him I was waiting for him to come pick it up. He told me he would be over soon to take a look at it. "Bring the money, cause you're gonna definitely want it," I told him.

As soon as he got to the house and saw the car, he took me with him to the bank. "Let's go," the minister said. "I don't need to test drive anything I'm buying from you, Bobby." We went to the bank, he gave me the cash, I signed over the title, and the car was gone not even by lunch time.

I am overly amazed! And I can tell you—that which I have spoken, I have lived. You have to speak your destiny in confidence. You can't allow any obstacle to come in between you and your success. Write the vision. Make it clear.

CHAPTER 12
CONQUERING THE SEEMINGLY UNCONQUERABLE

Many could say: 'I'm throwing in the towel, I've had enough, I can't go any further, that's absolutely too difficult for me.' Those statements to your psyche could have powerful interpretations for your brain. If we equate our brain to our stomach, we will remember too many sweets will cause our stomachs to hurt. Too much fried chicken with baked macaroni and cheese will do the same. This is not a good feeling at all. We would be tossing and turning all night. I'm sure you remember those times.

The brain is a delicate and sensitive instrument in our bodies. It works even when we are asleep. It also works even when I'm not thinking about it working. In church they call it 'Wonderworking' power. It is important to know this, and give it wholesome information just like we give wholesome food to our digestive system. Not caring for the brain will cause the brain to send signals that will disturb your body's actions and reactions. The brain operates on enough energy to power a 10 watt light bulb and that's even when you are asleep. When one has a prolonged gloomy outlook on so many things in their life, this negativity can and will cause your brain to lack the ability to reason and form memories; intrinsically pulling your brain's data and practically dissolving it. Another study reported in the Journal of American Academy of Neurology found that cynical thinking also produces a greater dementia risk. With that we must know that words and thoughts have power.

Upon approaching things that seem to be difficult and not attainable, we all need to be careful of how we think at that moment. Lions don't always win with loudness and strength. Sometimes they win with being still, watching, and thinking. With this as one of my guiding light measuring sticks, I suggest that you please read this chapter in stillness and meditate.

The pitfalls in life can be worrisome, at the least. They can propel medical numbers to go sky high or plummet so low that the unnecessary happens, and illness begins to run rampant.

I was at the church I attended with my wife, and there was a young lady there who was very established in politics and well known within the political arena. She came up one day and spoke to me. She told me she saw a building on Burnside Avenue in Inwood, NY. She suggested to me that maybe I should go look at it because at the time, I was teaching music in my home and traveling to different homes of families to give their students lessons.

Elaina and I were interested, and we trusted the woman's judgment. We went by and looked in. The building was empty and it wasn't very well taken care of. I turned to Elaina, and all I said was, "This is going to cost a lot of money."

I recognized how much work and how time consuming it would be for me to build the cabinets and soundproof the rooms. The only way I could do this was if I could do it without any struggling. I went into the office next door and spoke to an Orthodox Jewish man. I introduced myself to him. He told me he didn't own the space but that he could give me the phone number of the gentleman who did.

I went outside, called the number, and spoke to the owner. "Hey, Mr. Ains," I began. "I'm sitting outside of your building, and I am interested in the space." I told him who I was and my vision. He asked me how I was doing and I told him, 'I'm doing better than good and better than most. Today I am doing better than that.' He asked me where I came up with that saying and I told him it was from inside of myself, because I had made it up on the spot. "I would like to convert this space into a music school," I continued. I told him when I would be available later in the week to take a look inside. He said there was no need to make future plans. He had the gentleman from the other office give me his spare key so I could go inside. I knew then it was going to be mine.

We went inside and I saw Elaina, with her big smile, behind the counter. The chiropractic rooms, which had been out of commission since the last operation had moved elsewhere, were perfect for small studios and rooms to teach students in. I envisioned a recording studio in the largest room. There would be a 'Mommy and Me' section in another area. When I went back next door to return the key, I was met with another miracle. "Mr. Ains told me to tell you to keep the key."

"What?" I said.

"Mr. Ains told me to tell you to keep the key," the gentleman repeated. I went back in that afternoon, and I started walking out the place with my feet because I didn't have measuring tape with me. I called my cousin Perry who builds studios. It was the end of spring and by September, I had about 40-50 people there celebrating. We had food from the church and there was a big sign outside for 3 weeks that said, 'Coming Soon...' I asked what we were going to call the place. Keynote Music Center seemed perfect to us.

Before I knew it people were signing up. I had so many students coming in that I needed to start hiring teachers. We taught violin, viola, cello, bass, upright bass, trumpet, sound reinforcement, and we had drum and piano lessons. A 16 year old Italian girl who lived around the corner became the first drum teacher. She came in one day and showed us how well she played, and we hired her on the spot to give lessons. My friend Derrick Wright, Timothy Wright's son, gave drum lessons also. We had eleven teachers and my wife handled all of the scheduling and accounting. We rented pianos from Yamaha, and three were brand new that we owned.

Then Hurricane Sandy hit.

The closer I got to the school, the more trees I saw in the street. I finally got to my music school, and when I opened the door the keyboards were floating. All the amps were ruined, the upright bass was broken, and the equipment in the sound room was destroyed.

A month later, people started pouring in and giving me money and information. I called Derrick Wright and told him I had lost everything. I told him that all that I had was gone. "Do you have an old drum set I can borrow until I can get some drums?" I asked. He wouldn't allow me to borrow anything. At the time he was touring with Adele in Europe. He sent me a new drum set. My friendship with Derrick wasn't a fluke. His father, Timothy Wright, was a musician that I must have booked 15 times. He came to my lot to buy cars from me, and he would take with him two of his boys. Derrick was one of those boys. I was making an impression on him when he was a child that low and behold allowed for a positive connection between the two of us when he was an adult.

How many times have you looked at something and said to yourself, "Wow, I think I could have done that"? Yet, you never tried. What about that dish you couldn't pull yourself to try to cook—now it's one of your signature plates. Countless stories like this, in all facets of life, take precedence over fear and doubt. If you attempt something and follow through, life happens, and you are brought to another level of your existence. No matter what happens next, you are closer to where you want to be more than ever before. Stop for a moment and enjoy how far you have come. There is a past version of you that was wishing they could be you today and doing what you are doing. If you feel there is still more to be done or you want to change around some activities, you are better off today than you were yesterday to make those adjustments.

I remember playing piano for this church, and there was a woman who sat not far from me. Most people spoke unfavorably about her tone, her sound, and her pitch, yet my wife told her to sign up at my music school. My job was to teach whomever came in my room, and I did without question. My wife was totally in charge of the school I built for her. She had a staff to handle, scheduling to work out, payroll to administer, tuition to collect, and rent and bills to pay. All I was was a teacher like the other ten music instructors that I hired there. When this new student entered my room, I was shocked beyond dismay. However, my wife knows best.

I remember one time my wife said to me, "Bobby, the entire church can tell when you like or don't like something."

"EJ, that's impossible," I told her. "I'm very aware of how I keep my face when I smile and when I lift my eyebrows up."

Again, she repeated, "Bobby, the entire church can tell when you like or don't like something. I'm sure you're going to do a great job with this student."

I worked with this lady for about three months. She became my special project. She was very nice, sweet, and determined to get the most out of me that you could get, and I gave it to her. Diaphragmatic breathing, match this note, vowels, match this note, and on and on and on; I knew it was inside of her. It had to be found and brought out. The answer is always within. We both labored until she was able to sing a scale. Then she sang a melody in my room. Week after week she would come, week after week we would work. She never gave up, and I never gave in. Oh, how well do I remember that service she sang in. She sent a note up to do her first solo. It was beautiful and pleasurable to the ear. I did all I could do not to smile or cry. It was not about me. It was about that which is in me and that which I was able to pull out of her to do the same. The song says, "What a difference a day makes, 24 little hours." In our case, three little months. What if she had given up or thrown in the proverbial towel and said, 'This is all I'm gonna do and that's it.' What if she would've said, 'To God be the glory—He knows my heart.' Better still, what if she would've said, 'So what—pray for me.' She reached that place in her life, and she wanted to do it regardless of what anyone else said. Yes, she did, and so can you.

Conquering the seemingly unconquerable—the most important part of those words is 'seemingly.' My question to you is: what is your 'seemingly?' What are those hurdles in your life that you think cannot be achieved? Do you have any 'Mission Impossibles?' Every time I saw that movie on TV the result was VICTORY. There's a song that I heard in church that says, 'Victory, victory shall be mine, if I hold my peace and let the Lord fight my battle, victory, victory shall be mine.' The end result is always that the bad guys get conquered. The end result is created by strong preparation mixed with tenacity and mastery. Those parts together equal success.

What if I told you that the thing you are going through will no longer be an issue within a certain length of time? Do you think it has a time limit stamped on it that you can change? That which is your battle, has a date of defeat on it. It's on your tongue—speak it with confidence.

My friend Timothy Wright, wrote a song and it says, "Trouble Don't Last Always." Therefore, it's time to count your good days, and know that you have the power to shake dirt, negative thoughts, bad debt, and sickness off of your back and into the pit. Well, I say to step on it. Step on the baggage. Step on it more and more. Step until you have enough under your feet to step out of your dilemma and march forward onto victory.

Know that victory is yours. It's time to dance like nobody's watching. The power of spoken word, undergirded with our faith, propelled with tenacity and mastery in any given subject area, will put us at ease as we earn straight A's in Success 101. Each time we succeed, and with every victory, we move on to another master class of accomplishments. I want you to know that every accomplishment strengthens your confidence muscles. It is not good to jump into the middle of a giant problem, yet you can most certainly go 'poco a poco,' or little by little. Sitting down and evaluating the mission is the beginning of your end. Once we look at the concern, we can write out the ending. The process will provide light to you in your tunnel. The unconquerable goal or feat is now a visible plan of action. Soon, you'll see it all through a different lens.

Imagine being home one night and watching your favorite sports team playing in the finals. They are losing at first, but at the end, you are elated to watch them win the championship. What a sense of jubilation! The next morning, your oldest son wakes up to see the amazing game you recorded the night before. As the game is being played, you watch as your son gets disappointed because your team was losing at the beginning; but you know the secret. You know they are going to win! Well, in life, some situations may look bleak. They may be less than inviting, and they may cause some feelings of anguish or failure. In this mindstate, the big look bigger, and then bigger things become humongous; humongous now becomes mammoth. With all of the worry, we only enlarge the scenario. However, you have the end in sight—and it is all good.

Never look at the adversities in life as bigger than you are. You are life. You are special. You are one-of-a-kind. You are full of greatness. See it for what it is: a passing storm, water under the bridge, or, better still, just a moment in time.

And this too shall pass.

Behind every dark cloud there is a silver lining. In the words of Charles R. Swindoll, "Life is 10% what happens to me and 90% of how I react to it." Go forth and conquer victories. Victory shall be mine. . . No! Victory is mine.

CHAPTER 13
OVERCOMING THE ODDS

Everywhere you go there is trouble. Everywhere you go there's something that bothers you: difficulties on every hand and adversities everywhere. These calamities can affect you directly as they have for me and members of my immediate family and friends. I've gone through seemingly insurmountable hardships difficult enough to knock me off of my feet. At times I found myself taking five steps forward and ten steps backwards within a mere two days. It seems that the odds were stacked up against me on every hand. The blizzard was blowing in my face while I was trying to move forward. Concrete walls were in front of me on every turn. However, with resolution, flexibility, and an upward thrust of motion, despite the hills, and in spite of the slippery roads, and unpredictable weather conditions, I passed all of the nays—I made it. In the words of Curtis Mayfield, "Keep on pushing."

The answer within teaches us that there is always a way out of no way. The answer within will cut down hedges and make straight your path. I have seen it done in my personal life. This is not something that I'm reading about. This is not something someone told me about. This is my story. This is my song. I don't brag or bask in my setbacks. I just reflect on knowing that all things are possible as long as I can focus because with my attention, I can always find my way. Even if I was knocked down the words of Les Brown are seared into my mind: 'If I can look up, I can get up.'

Setbacks are more than discouraging experiences that slow down your progress. For me the cause of them has become a motivating phenomenon, something that enables me to see the glory within. My friends often think I'm absurd when they see a setback or failure occur in my life and witness me laugh, shout, and jump. When these problems arise, I'm saying, 'Glory!' I differ from many. When setbacks or failures occur, I'm happy. Why? Because every failure, every setback that comes out of me, ushers me closer to my goal.

I was in Manhattan one evening on 57th street, and as everyone knows, 57th is famous for having many high-end and designer stores. I went into Steinway Pianos with the sincere idea that I wanted to purchase a few pianos for my music school. I stood at the door, being 6 foot 3 and 190 pounds, and I looked at these little kids all jumping around and slamming on the keys. I was standing around waiting for someone to help me, because I was actually interested in making the fairly large purchase that day...

Finally, I walked all the way into the store and I saw a sales person. "Excuse me," I began. "I have been standing in the store for 20 minutes and no one has come to help me." They responded with their apologies and told me they didn't see me. All the same, they asked how they could help. I told them I was interested in making a purchase of two pianos.

"Can you play?" they asked. I nodded. I moved closer to one of their pianos. I could tell they seemed hesitant for some reason as I sat down. I played the first few measures of the Rachmaninoff Prelude in C Sharp minor which was a big deal. Everyone in the store ceased their escapades. Even the children stopped what they were doing. They all started to walk themselves toward where I was playing. I stood up. "That's okay, thank you... I came in here to get two pianos for my music school and apparently this is not for me."

I knew that these pianos were going to cost me an excess of $80,000 dollars a piece. I walked out of the store and went back to Keynote. When I got there, I called Steinway, and I told them about the school. I told their representative over the phone that I would love to see what programs they offered for music schools teaching children. The spokeswoman said that they did in fact have such programs and that they would come to see our operations.

Two weeks after that, I had three brand new Steinway pianos for my music school and we were even endorsed by Steinway. We were allowed to use their emblem in our window and on our stationery. Ironically, my initial idea was that I was going to go buy two pianos and spend my own money on them, but since I wasn't treated very nicely, plans changed and now I had three pianos without needing to even spend a dime. That uncomfortable moment actually propelled me in the direction of a better reality.

Every time it does not work out properly, I am a strong believer that at that given time the result is for a specific reason or multiple reasons. After experiencing this repeatedly and consistently in my life, I can honestly feel gratitude and keep my happiness intact no matter the situation, because I know these 'mishaps' get me closer to my goals. I realize that there is a certain amount of noise inside of every job and every plan. Certain obstacles must be dealt with accordingly. While you figure out and deal with the right solutions, look at these hairy situations as opportunities. Everytime something does not work out correctly, you get some practice in life while trying to exercise this particular ideal that no matter what—this all gets you closer and closer to your goal.

Moreover, the determination to pursue one's goals in the face of adversity is a driving force that propels individuals beyond the odds. When faced with formidable challenges, it is the unyielding determination to persevere that sets the stage for victory. Whether it's pursuing education in the face of financial hardship, striving for a career breakthrough amidst fierce competition, or advocating for change in the midst of opposition—determination fuels the journey towards triumph.

With that, my motivation to continue on in my direction in the midst of the pain, the anguish, and the agony propels me even more so. It's like a giant windmill tied to my back and pushing me straight forward. I actually believe that sometimes it pushes me in the directions that I may not have even planned. Yet, when I look back over my life and all that I've done, I still shout in the words of my friend, the late Timothy Wright, "Trouble don't last always."

The road has been rough, going has been tough, and hardship has been there for me. No, I never lived where I had to go outside to an outhouse. There never was 8, 9, or 10 of us in a two bedroom apartment. I've never had to wear shoes with cardboard nailed on the bottom because of a hole in the sole. I've always had something to eat more than I could digest. I do realize that my hurdle may not be the same as your hurdle. Pain is pain no matter who's receiving it. The answer within has resolved so many things in my life. I could title this book, 'Look Where God Has Brought Me From.'

When I was not focused properly, the road could feel long and excruciating. It was a long road, but it was the roadtrip of a lifetime. Where He brought me from would encompass only a part of my overall story. The lousy times would only encompass a very miniscule part of my life, therefore I trust whole-heartedly in the voice that talks with me and tells me, 'I am with you.'

CHAPTER 14
I HAVE ONLY JUST BEGUN

You finally made it. Look! You're at that phase of life where you have your own place to rest your head. A place you can call your own. What is this that I see? Is that a second home you can use or rent out depending on the weather? Yes.

The thermostat for the heat is in your hand now and not the landlord's. A car or two are in the garage and maintained well; what a pleasure it is to decide which one you want to drive depending on where you're going. Vacations once every two or three years if that, but now you can do one, two, or a few vacations a year—just turn the globe and start picking.

You have a job that you are fully comfortable with. No more sweating when the boss comes around. Children are living on their own comfortably or in college and away at school. Both closets are full and "the living is easy."

You look around, and not only you, but your immediate friends are doing well too. Sometimes, without even noticing, you find out that you lost the desire to feel that you are less fortunate.

Many years before this story begins, you feel like this prosperity is lifetimes away. Do you remember when the entire family lived in that one apartment with maybe two bedrooms or no more than three? When someone was cooking, you could smell the food all over the building. What about the time when there were only fans, and air conditioning was a luxury item only enjoyed while riding in buses and trains? If you had one unit it was a blessing, now every room is comfortably cool in the sweltering heat of the summer.

Maybe to you it still feels special to go to the movie theater or to buy a pair of sneakers, because you remember a time when most likely kids had maybe one pair of shoes with one suit and two dress shirts or one nice dress and one pair of shoes. When you appreciate what you have and are not one to take things for granted, the road you're traveling on in life starts to rise to correlate with the weightlessness of your heart.

Going outside to jump rope, play 'Skelly,' or 'Red Light, Green Light, 123' was an easy way to have fun; however, when you played these games in such a blissful state, I guarantee you did not find yourself asking: 'What's next?' Now in our adulthood, we can't help but at random times, unknown as to why, hear that small voice inside asking, 'Where do we go from here?'

The thing about life is that it is so very easy to become complacent, stagnated, and unmotivated. This usually happens because of lack of insight and trusting or acting on foresight. I believe that one of the worst things is when you are too comfortable, and you fall into a slumber, becoming stuck in the same place for five years, and not know. It's good to take inventory every few months as to where you are and where you were. You're on the right path, and you can not show up late for the culminating experiences of your existence.

You naturally are seeking answers to find out your future and what is next for you because of fear and feeling as if you are running out of time. Life can move so fast and we make so many decisions each day. We can often gloss over how much we have grown, what we have improved on, and how close we are from closing whatever gaps we were trying to make headway on toward breaking cycles. I will always say on repeat to get it off your chest, out of only your mind, and to put it on paper. There is a reason why your mathematics teacher always reminded the class to show their work! Your life is intricate and complex, putting down where you've been and where you are headed on paper always helps you to visualize better the logic toward where you are headed. Cry when you need to, release the heaviness on your soul, but at some point, let the answer within, with all of its accuracy, soothe you. You are always in an eternal embrace with the ultimate pattern maker and weaver of your life. Your brain is designed fearfully and thoughtfully to recognize the template, run the data, and print the analysis. Your life's greatest research is YOU, and you are going to win the laureate and Nobel Prize in your own unrepeatable category.

Do you look at people and shame them in your mind? If not, stop doing it to yourself. If you do, stop doing it to them, and allow the peace of the unknown to wash over you. No one is down and out for the count, and no one knows how their life can potentially change over the course of one year.

These positives and well intentioned practices will enable you to keep your compass sharp and calibrated toward your cardinal directions. There's no time to stop. Stopping is not an option. Yes, you must get rest and plenty of it, but you will not stop. You will keep your mind active, and continue to keep your body moving. An object in motion stays in motion. Always be in the midst of working or developing an idea.

Whatever success or love you have right now, say to yourself: 'I have only just begun.' In order to have a long, healthy life always find yourself working on the amount of love you can show yourself and others. Love your ideas and support the ideas of others. Short term plans, which can be three months to a year, can help you stay patient while you're waiting for those long-term ideas, 5 to 8 years out, to unfurl. As soon as you come closer and closer to closing on a cycle or a term, make sure you work and let another one start. These short and long term goals and ideas keep your brain concentrated on your life's work and focused on results, ultimately pushing you toward your celebratory moments and the meeting of your agenda. Be happy in the moments you find yourself wondering how this will all transpire. Be grateful you're asking yourself 'how' instead of thinking that your milestones will not come to pass. You will make it, and you can bask in your glory now.

It's fine that you have accomplished so much that you can't even remember back to the beginning stage. Don't fall into guilt trips. You are allowed to have nice things. If you have it, you've earned it. Stop thinking that because you have something you must have stolen it and that it's not good. It is good to have and to have in abundance. Yet with all that you've accomplished, always remember, you've only just begun. One would ask, how is that possible? And the answer is easy, because there's so much MORTGAGE to accomplish. There's so much more to do. There's so much more to give. If you stop where you are now and don't do anything else, then where is the excitement? The zest for living? Where is the interest to move, to go, to do? If this goal and those mountains weren't there, what would you be doing? You've conquered some of the mountains? Great! Now enjoy some rest, restock on your energy supplies, secure the reserves, and go for Mount Kilimanjaro!

There are still flights to be taken and by now you have flown many of them. I say, fly higher and longer. Become a pilot whose flight plan is your greatest self. Let the black box, simultaneously recording everything in the cockpit, be the makings of your own story and future publication to share.

If cooking meals is something you enjoy doing, why not decide to call up some family members and invite them over to your home no matter how small you think the room is and cook for your entire family. Get a bigger view on what makes life worth living. In times when you were feeling discomforted, now feel at a place where you can think past those low feelings of self doubt and shame. Feel higher, feed more, do more—it is a song to sing, and you wrote the lyrics and the melody. In a world with so many casting stones, where people normalize negative behavior; justifying pettiness as being alright for others to partake in—help people to propel to their greatness. As long as you know there's more growth and look deep inside yourself, you'll remember you've only just begun. You've only just begun to tap the surface of your deeper success.

'Bobby, I'm retired. I've done my 20, my 30, my 40 years on my job. It's time for me to sit back in my rocking chair and get my remote control and enjoy the fruits of my labor.' My answer is, NO! No. It's time for you to teach and time for you to demonstrate an easier way to do what you did. Life is not over until the fat lady sings. Even if she does, as long as there's another breath to breathe, another note to grab, another melody to pull out then retirement cannot hold you back.

Now is the time to get more, to have more, and to do more. Don't get down and get stuck thinking you've had your best days. Stand in your ultimate form and just like that—stand the test of time. You have a wealth of knowledge inside of you. You have experience that needs to be shared. You've been places that some people would only dream about. You built monuments that will be recognized and shine. Now it's time for another one, but it still needs to be sculpted. You have the energy and the help you need.

Always remember that the seed is in your hand. Soil is beckoning your name to till it. That young boy's mind and that young girl's mind are waiting like sponges to absorb the wisdom only you can give.

Yes! You've only just begun. So now go forth and onward. You don't have to look deep inside yourself while being confused and still waiting to decide which part of yourself you want to bring out— be the total sum of who you are.

I remember at the age of 11, my mother had me teaching all of her friends from the hospital. They were all 33 to 43 years older than me and for some reason I could hear voices that needed tuning up. I had this high-pitched voice as a little boy, and I was directing grown men and women. I found out the adults listening to me as I was teaching them harmony had thought at first that I couldn't possibly know what I was doing or what I was talking about. They thought I was a joke, but pretty soon they witnessed and experienced the same awe inspiring phenomenon that I did. As I look back, I realize that I was purely and innocently responding to what was inside of me and it didn't matter my age or my pip squeak voice.

I remember probably at the age of five playing Fats Domino, 'I Found my Thrill on Blueberry Hill.' I'm 5 or 6 years old playing and singing that song written by someone in their 30s. I was a little boy and this was when I had never taken piano lessons. Fats Domino was born in 1928. He was 30 years old—what am I doing knowing a 30 year old man's song and being able to play it? I would ask my mother at church if I could go to the bathroom. I would sneak from the top level to the basement level and play the piano. People would find me down there and yell at me to stop messing with the keys and to come back upstairs.

I began to sing songs and try to play them. I had no piano teacher yet and zero musical background. It just came to me and came out of me. Six years later, I was teaching people how to sing, how to do harmony, and how to enunciate their words. It became second nature to me. It was not a joke. . . It was serious. I had a mission at 11 years old.

I always liked to teach this world to sing and be in perfect harmony. I enjoyed it a little and soon enough it became my avenue of fun. When others were out playing basketball, I wanted to play the piano. God had placed my gifts within me at an early age. I had to grow into them. My gifts were always bigger than myself, my imagination, and my feet. I could not walk in my gifts.

I remember a story about a boy genius. He said that his life was not good and that it was particularly miserable, because everything he said was always right. He could also do things like mathematical equations before the teacher worked them out with the class in order to solve them. He ended up feeling isolated and alone. I'm far from a genius, but I was touched by the hand of God coming out of my mothers womb. Many people don't know that my mother's first child died and that's why she was very overprotective of me. The doctor told her before I was born that I was either going to die or that my coming would be a very successful birth.

When I touched the piano it was like the missing link, but I did not only touch the piano: I heard the harmony and the melody. At Sunday school when I would sing, I was not singing as a 5, 6, 7, or 8 year old child. I was singing like I was part of the main choir. That was inside of me. Then wisdom became part of my life, but the shoes were still too big to wear. I know when I say that the answer within is not just putting ink to paper, it's putting your life to paper.

The answer is within. If it's in me, then it's within you. I am no greater than you, and you are no greater than I.

CHAPTER 15
SUDDENLY

Many times in our lives we find ourselves looking at things and not understanding how we got there and why we've been there for so long. There have been certain situations that I became so numb to that they became a part of who I was. I would walk around slowly, shoulders bent, and dragging my feet. I couldn't dress myself properly. I was just being and becoming one with the negative environment around me.

I knew that there had to be a better way. I knew that there must be light somewhere. And there it was! After deciding to create love in my heart, things began to happen for me—and not slowly! Suddenly, my bills were paid. Suddenly, my mortgage was paid off. Suddenly, the disobedient child followed my directions. This can and will happen for you. Your flow state is your destiny. Imagine your story. . . Suddenly, you start waking up in the morning with more energy. Suddenly, you become less downtrodden from all the past memories and heartbreaks. Suddenly, you are able to rest on the more simple and pleasant things in life. Suddenly, your husband or wife comes along.

How does it happen? It happens when you do not give up, or give in, but when you hold out strong—when you become a winner. How do we allow ourselves that golden opportunity? You speak life and friendship to yourself. Suddenly, you hear a whisper in your ear saying that things will improve. And suddenly, they do.

However, that 'suddenly' may take too long, or that 'suddenly' may not be strong enough. Many people walk, and walk, and walk, and just when they are about to get to *suddenly*. . . they throw up their hands.

Your 'suddenly' is truthfully right around the corner. Your 'suddenly' is calling forth your name. Your 'suddenly' is right in front of you. No, don't give up!

How many times have people tried to bake that perfect cake? How many times have you tried to figure out that complex math equation? But suddenly, it happens.

Maybe you've gone to the doctor numerous times and your health has not changed. Perhaps you thought to yourself, 'I won't get better,' or 'I will be in this state forever.' But then suddenly, your health improves. How? Because you did not give up.

We cannot allow the place we are in in life to be the place where we stay put. You may know you do not want to be there, but you have become so numb that you don't even consider the situation anymore.

Sometimes we lay in a stupor. We find ourselves doing the same thing day after day and week after week. Decades later, we look up and we are still in the same place. And we don't allow the 'suddenly' to break through.

It is possible for you to remain where you are for a lifetime and never develop your 'suddenly,' never develop your breakthrough, and not develop to the place where you need to be. Sometimes you can't even see it, because you have been in the same state for so long. Just like the fleas, you allowed the negative to impact your vision. Sometimes you have to move yourself away from yourself and be like Little Anthony in the Imperials when he said, "I'm on the outside looking in."

You have to step outside of yourself. And tell yourself: "Self, it's time for a breakthrough! Self, it's time for me to climb this mountain. Self, it's time for me to get those things in life I'm supposed to have." You suddenly will be at your good times. Reach out and touch what you have. It's yours because you spoke it. Suddenly it is close, although it may seem far away. Your 'suddenly' can even be today, if you start to see the design and pattern within all things good. There's a reason they say: 'Happiness grows.' Put your mind on your good news and the people in your life who make you feel calm. Make sure you treat others the way you treat yourself and vice versa. Imagine the advice you would give to your most beloved companion. Please talk to yourself like that and believe it. The same way you would believe the advice you would give to a sister, brother, son, or daughter.

In order to bring it closer, you must walk that extra mile. It's there waiting on you. You will not stay the same. Things will not remain as they are now. You will have your breakthrough. You will see your finances improved. You will be able to see your child grow. You will see your spouse being the best they can be. Better still, you will be the best spouse you can be. . . That will surely make the process better.

So, let's make it happen. How soon?

Suddenly.

CHAPTER 16
MY SHORTEST CHAPTER

MY FIRST REJECTION AFTER EJ.

Can you believe it's been 7 years and 7 months since EJ left me and went to glory? For the last year my children and my sister have been telling me it is time to meet and greet. I continued to say to them that EJ left the barline way too high for anyone to enter my life. I rest on the fact that I am okay as long as my daughters are okay. However, these girls are my strongest push, so when they tell me to do something, it's a bit stronger than a slight nudge.

I remember prior to meeting EJ I wrote down exactly what I wanted in a woman. The song says, "I got my mind made up and I won't turn back, I want to see my savior one day." Well I wanted to see my wife one day. I had waited and waited until EJ moved next door and the rest was history—the next 18 years of heaven were made just for me. She was a wife and she was unmeasurable.

A year ago, I saw a beautiful lady standing and talking to someone.

All I could say was that mine eyes had seen the glory of the coming of a–wife. However, I dare not say a word to her. I went on my way and continued to enjoy my life. I have seen her twice since that time, just in passing; we both would say hello and keep on moving our separate ways. All I knew is her beauty was so deep inside of her until each time she would smile or open her mouth to speak and then it was blinding with her aura and her meekness. Let us all know that meekness often is a sign of weakness. However, it is a quality that describes someone who is humble, gentle, and who has a willingness to yield to God's will.

I am a different type of guy, therefore half-dressed, flirtatious, and overdoing makeup is not my desire. I know I can not duplicate EJ, yet I still have my personal enticements. I really am not looking, truth be told, but it was good to see what I saw.

As time went on and on, eventually all that was gone. She never knew what I felt and I, being new to the art of dating, was totally in her rearview not able to say a word. I attempted one more time. In my regular fashion, I invited her to my annual Christmas caroling party. When I saw her sitting apart from everyone else, I thought it was a sign I should continue the conversation with her. We continued to communicate until she told me that she was recently divorced and wanted to spend time with her children. We remain friends, in the words of Bette Midler, "From a Distance."

I never had a desire to forge ahead to find a mate. I just wanted to live a life that was pleasing to God and that would make my three daughters proud of their dad. Onward and upward I march to conquer my next battle.

On top of it all, everything in my life has come to me. I never had to rap or go through all the things that guys went through to have fun. My music and my name always did it for me. I just stood back and watched how life unfolded right in front of me, even to the place of always finding a parking spot no matter where or what time. Actually, God has spoiled me, and I love it.

CHAPTER 17
GOING IN THE WRONG DIRECTION TO FIND THE RIGHT PATH

I found myself going around in circles trying to find the things that I wanted in life. For so long, while I was spinning around and around, I missed the things that I wanted because of the things that I was not doing. Sometimes you can work so hard and so diligently trying to make it work until you become so at a loss to see that it is still not working.

I had to pull myself up by my own bootstraps and question myself on why my life was daunting and confusing. I was getting lost at times in the shadows, and it wasn't until I discovered the logic within my behavior patterns that my effectiveness kicked in. The problems weren't stemming from the things that I was doing; instead they came about because of the things that I was not doing.
My lack of cognizance left me with empty voids that I haphazardly tried to fill myself. When I filled myself with the superficial, I was then led to understand what I needed to do to greater serve myself. I was able to see how I was overlooking the inevitable. I was jumping over my own destination. I was paying no mind to the answers that I needed and choosing quick fixes that wouldn't amount to much in effect.

It is easy to get discouraged, because you're chasing after something that is not. Yet you work so hard at it, you pray for it, and you meditate trying to get it. Guess what? It's not there and it took me a long time to find out. . .

I was going in the wrong direction trying to find the right answer. Oh, how well I can remember when I had to come to a halt in the midst of sweating, in the midst of agony, and in the midst of screaming out for help. 'Bobby! Stop! It's not there…' I came to the realization that what I was trying to find was continuously evading me, because I was not focused in the right place.

How many of you have worked countless hours, days, weeks, and sometimes years to no avail. I say, pull over, get out of that car, and look toward a different direction. Sometimes you may even have to go back a little bit in order to get your momentum going again; this time in the right direction. And if it's not the right direction? Well, at least you gained more knowledge to apply to the next situation you're in to make your goal come out as a win.

It's not about doing more—it's about doing more, *correctly*. I remember one of my piano students worked a whole week practicing a scale that I gave them. I told them the G major scale is played with the exact same fingering as a C major scale, however, it has a sharp in the key which is F. My student worked that entire week practicing the G major scale for two octaves to impress me. However, they left out the sharp. They played F natural. That means that all the practicing they did, all the sacrificing they did, and all the time that was applied to play the scale correctly was in vain. How many of you have worked diligently on your quest only to find out that nothing you were doing was working? How many of you have put in blood, sweat, and tears to make that which you wanted to grow not even begin to develop? It could be nursing, carpentry, or drawing up those drafts that you want to create only to find out that all that you did was not correct.

When you're working on something I always say, 'write the vision.' Write it clearly, look at it, and think about it. Your inner voice will begin to speak to you, don't allow your emotions to give you the answers to match what's real. My student ended up having to go back and retrain that muscle memory so that they would be able to execute that scale correctly. We too must do the same sometimes. It's not that you're not working, but it's very possible you are working too hard in another direction and, therefore, not at all efficiently. Your training and your memory, whether it's your brain memory or your muscle memory, all needs to be in check.

We must push ourselves in the right direction. That is what will give us the desires of our heart. Our goals are not far; it's just that we must know the right way to get to them. Once we reach a goal post, the joy that we have will be unspeakable.

A sigh of relief is the outward expression for a job well done. Nevertheless, prior to getting to that final stage, never become self-satisfied with artificial victories. We must step on the outside of our comfort zone and start working vigorously on our dreams from the ground up. It doesn't matter if we are attempting to conquer a new position, placement in a new school, or working to break a habit that has previously kicked us in the butt.

In the words of my deceased father, with a second grade education, he said to me upon feeling my discontentedness once, "Boy, a little kick in the butt in the right direction is sometimes good for you." Please remember in order to break through barriers, those same barriers will in turn end up being your assistance and a great help to you.

You must do more than what you're doing. Let's go to places that you have not gone. Sometimes you have to move. You must encircle yourself with new people. If you're the best in that group then it's time for you to leave. 'Look up and down the row that you're sitting in, and if you find you're the best person in that row, it's time for you to sit in another row. . .' Pastor Taylor said that. If you've been praying the same prayer over and over, it's okay to say a different one. Stop being redundant, stop begging, and start believing. I believe the things that I ask God for. While I'm asking He's already paced out the motions, so before I get off my knees, the things that I pray for are already done. I am no different than anyone who reads this book.

I remember when I was playing at this church and for some reason despite all of the accolades that I was receiving in the beginning, the good vibes began to dissipate. I do not live off of financial rewards; I live off of 'thank you's. One of the 5 love languages is appreciation. Receiving the words 'thank you,' along with genuine compliments, and the expression of gratitude are soothing to the soul. The spirit within you will tap into the person whose spirit is giving. One day these praises just stopped and turned into public critiques and public shaming. For some reason at this particular job, I kept going round and round searching for ways to appease. I eventually began to see what was for me was not there, but I was too interested in getting the "okay" from the supervisors. I was unable to get the message from myself saying that it was time to go. I remember the song of Billy Preston, 'Will you go around in circles? Nothing from nothing leaves nothing'. . . Finally one day, I wrote down my resignation and I read it publicly. I read it in a way that I could never get that position back, because I wanted to make sure that my 'so long' was a 'good-bye.' I left that place and moved on to another venue that paid me four times the salary while doing about eight times less work than what I was doing where I had come from. I say this not to boast in any form or fashion. Sometimes you can be going in the wrong direction and a kick in the butt will help you. I found myself pulling away until I found myself going in a better direction.

CHAPTER 18
DON'T YOU DARE STOP

Many times we search and search, long and far, and make turbulence and ruckus in our ordeals trying to find that which is already at hand. We have programmed ourselves to believe that anything and everything we need is somewhere between the clouds and the circumference of our planet. We believe that the results of our query require blood, sweat, and tears in order to come to fruition.

What we are, what we see, and what is truly at hand can become murky and hard to make out due to fear and doubt. When you surround yourself with people that have the idea that if you want to play hard, you must work hard, that's what you are going to believe. This idea lends itself to the idea that if you are seeking an answer you don't know off hand, you will irrevocably believe you must bury yourself into major research, pain, and anguish, to gain the answer you seek. When you feel the negativity coming on, ground yourself back to your inner knowing. That answer within is the voice of the creator and designer of your life. Listen and walk in the sunshine for the day. You will not forget the genuine love and befitting pureness you feel. This frequency will mend your heart, heal disease, and change not only your life for the better but will also assist others around you to live out their glory. As you become more suited to the light, the choice of which voice to listen to will become less of an option and more second nature.

Let's probe and see how close the finish line really is. Where is the victory flag? Better yet, where is the smile that hurts because you did it? Lets remember the song by Roberta Flack, 'The closer I get to you, the more it makes me feel.' That smile is yelling out your name just as much as you are seeking it in your quest. The flag of victory is waving back and forth trying to get your attention just as much as you are working to find it. That bold white finish line is there so you won't miss it as you approach the end of your final lap. Yes! It is all at hand and ready for you to move upward and forward. Keep moving and don't give up.

I stand on the fact that life is perplexing, to say the least. This does not mean that one must put themselves in a frenzy in order to sail on rough seas. My brother-in-law, Lloyd, taught me a pivotal lesson. One beautiful, sunny day toward the end of April, I was steering and captaining, 'STERLING,' the family boat with him. 'Bobby, don't go across the waves, ride with the tide, and then our boat will not rock,' he advised. I still use the same premise in navigating the hurdles of life. It does not take hard work to achieve a difficult task. It takes a mind that is steadfast and unmovable. When you're piloting a boat one direction and the waves are coming at you, it's a mistake to continue driving straight on vertically into the wake since they're still coming horizontally. This way of maneuvering will make everyone on the boat very uncomfortable and toss them around. If the waves are coming at you, you want to turn the boat parallel and gradually move yourself into the wave, so you're easing over them to your port or starboard side. You can have a cup of tea on the boat in the same conditions as before when you were getting thrown around and disgruntled. This way of thinking applies to us. Use your obstacles by letting them take you in a different direction. For example, sometimes you're driving to go home, and there's a big sign that says 'DETOUR: Don't go this way,' and you try to go around it thinking you can beat it by trying to ignore it. Now you're either in a maze or totally blocked off, because there was a reason for the detour in the first place, and if you had just turned and went with the grain instead of against it, you'd have already arrived home. Go with the signs, just take the detour. The detour is still taking you in the right direction just another way. 'Bobby, ride that wave'. . . I'll never forget that day or that advice.

To know the reality of who you are means you can be resourceful with what you are facing and experiencing. Teachers will appear to you along your way, quietly or loudly, nudging you to look at life in a more peaceful frame of mind. Let the challenges and obstacles do 96% of the work, while you live a prayerful life seeking and recognizing the answers that allow you to sit back and breathe sighs of relief. Think of yourself as a newborn child. The child belongs here. This world belongs to him or her. Would they be equipped or not equipped to handle the totality of the possibilities they could experience? The answer is you, just like the newborn, are built for your life. You were customized by God to make it to your finish line. If you weren't, you wouldn't have the desire in your heart. Not only are you similar to the newborn, you are God's child, young, innocent, and treasured in the eye of the Most High.

The compass is always within. As Earth Wind and Fire says, "Keep Your Head to the Sky." Just as one glimpse into your future is enough to cause your heart to soar to new heights, like a young fledgling bursting into the clear open blue, you can look toward the sun and see things in a different manner. We can tell the time and the direction we are traveling in by the position of the stars. *Per ardua ad astra*, through adversity to the stars. Let us determine the orientation and manner of our lives by the rays of exuberance emitting from our inner truth. Nothing is so far away that you can not reach it. In the words of Napoleon Hill, "If my mind can conceive it, and my heart can believe it, then I will achieve it."

Everything is at hand. Many times answers come in the night or on whispers of the wind, such as Andraé Crouch described: "It's those quiet times; they are so precious to me." Ideas strike us during phone calls, during a laugh, or during a speaker's presentation. My recommendation is to be on the lookout for the voice of wisdom. The answer within flows from heart to heart.

Don't you dare stop. The best is at hand and ready for you to receive.

____

____

____

My innate curiosity has always caused me to probe, investigate, and dive into possible resolutions. It has been through looking and searching for things that I have found the answer within.
In the words of Bob Dylan, 'The answer, my friend, is blowin' in the wind. The answer is blowin' in the wind.'

The Answer is Within.

END CREDITS

<u>Rev Dr. Johnny Youngblood</u>

Going to church for me at a tender age of 8 was mainly a meeting place for my friends and I. We were not allowed to hang in the streets. Therefore, church was our party. We would sing, usher, and eat 59 cent Hobbies from Benson Burgers on Eastern Parkway almost every Sunday. The fun never stopped. The pastor was a rather elderly, white haired minister named Reverend Adolphus Smith. I was too young to understand any of his messages, but I had to sit until he was finished. He was kind and loving to the members. Everyone respected and admired him. Yet, the messages were all over my little head. This is when I first heard hymns, negro spirituals, and anthems. I was different from all my friends; I liked the anthems, and they liked gospel music. Although the anthems did not have a hand clapping, foot stomping, pulsating rhythmic beat, they did have great musical harmonies, undergirded with syncopation, and funky overtones. I was unaware that this would be the beginning of me appreciating, "Music by the Masters."

Dr. Youngblood shocked the place into orbit and I was hooked.

This man revolutionized every aspect of my life. He never knew it. . . I did. This was the first time I could understand that 'I can,' because God and me are the majority. His message was so on point until not long thereafter he moved the church to another location. The membership grew rapidly and there was no room to hold the people. His messages empowered me to grow musically and to see the greater picture. I did not go with him because I was playing for another church. However, I continued to be elevated because of his gift of finessefully placed interpretations of God's words.

He had a way of bringing men to church and not talking down to us but rather lifting us up so that we could fly and walk on coals while not getting burned. Dr. Youngblood was intelligent and still is down to earth. He always treated me with the highest regards and respect; always assuring me of God's love.

Meeting Les Brown In my 30's

One morning, around 2 am, I was up watching TV and an infomercial with this brother talking about "You have greatness within you" and "Live your dreams" came on. I knew he was pointing directly toward me through the TV. I jumped out of my bed to see, in the words of Marvin Gaye, 'What's Going On?' My toes began to wiggle, and my heart began to beat with a strong sound of: 'I can understand.' I'd never felt this way before. My mind was like a sponge, and that very moment took me to my inner self and here I am today. . . Signed, Sealed, and Delivered.

I got up, called the number, and ordered his tapes. A month later I was brand new. It was too much for me to hold on to by myself. Therefore, I called the number again and left him a message to call me. He did. We talked as if we both knew each other for years. I remember our conversation vividly. It was another world being poured into me. I told him about being a New York promoter and how I wanted to bring him in. He agreed. We packed the venue, and now we are friends for life—not to mention he is my niece Dr. LaShai Williams's Godfather. He did the eulogy for my mother as well.

Stanley Brown

Stanley and I were always friends. I can not remember when we were not. His love for music of all genres and kind and respectful mannerisms kept me on point. No matter where he or I were, I was always treated with the highest regard. He played his behind off. When he was young, I would help him with his equipment getting to and fro. That was when we all first began. Since that time, he has been involved with Grammy Award winning artists. He played with 7 groups, and at any given time I would call him and ask him if he could write and help me with music. He would always take my phone calls and spend time with me.

Today he is a multidimensional artist, producer, and composer in the music industry.

Stanley has worked with many giants such as India Arie, Dru Hill, Bobby Brown, Hezekiah Walker, Donald Lawrence, and so many others. Yet we stay in contact to share good news, and he is always there for support.

Rev Dr. Clarence Norman Sr

The people who have come into my life amaze me. None were and are less than the other. This black historian filled my cup until it overflowed. The best part of our relationship was that I sat directly behind him every Sunday for 13 plus years. His intellect, along with his stories, were mind boggling. He took me to the stratosphere. He spoke with a paint brush. Every sentence was packed with colorful verbiage and electrifying power. When he walked into a room everyone knew it. He constantly said, "No one knows what's in your pocket… So walk like you got a million."

I've learned more from this man than anyone on earth. He taught me to be a leader without any fears. He paved a way for my businesses to grow exponentially. The people he has introduced me to are all powerful and respected amongst their peers. He appreciated great music of all types. This caused me to continue to learn, practice, and develop those around me for the Glory of God.

I remember one Sunday after church, I was terribly upset with all my staff. There were about 13 musicians that worked with me. I wanted to fire everyone. I went into his office with them and explained my plight. He acknowledged my position and my displeasure toward my staff. He then asked everyone to wait outside as he and I spoke like we always did. He said, "Bobby, if you want to fire everyone, I will back you. However, if one or two were to be let go, it would look like only they were wrong. Similarly, if the entire staff is let go then you would look bad and possibly lose the battle with the other choir members." Then he asked, "What are you going to do?" I replied that I would take them out for dinner and talk. Afterwards, I continued with my team. This is just one of many things I learned from this preacher.

I am so grateful for the years I sat under his tutelage.

Dr. Sharon Banks-Williams

She has always been a fire storm in my life. Because of her I've grown. She and my wife, Elaina, were always known as sisters. So when they got together, I was left out because of the bond they had. They shaped me, worked with me, and caused me to move forward to a level of greatness that I knew was inside of me but needed help to see.

My sister was driving around in a two seater Mercedes-Benz. She always had nice cars, because her husband always took good care of her, and I always would ask her if I could have it. She told me, 'when I got my life together.' She got me my first hardtop, two seater Benz. The hardest times I saw in her life was when her house burned down 3 days before Christmas. I was toe up and toe down, but I didn't want to show her I was struggling, because I wanted to be an anchor for her. The same answer inside of me is inside of her, and she was able to do much in her life that my mother instilled in us by always saying we are immeasurable resources.

Perry McNeil

Relatives are forced upon you. If you're my uncle it's because you are my mother's brother. If you're my cousin it's because you're my aunt's child. I have no choice in the matter, but I do have a choice if you are my friend or not. I chose Perry and he chose me. He was with me forever, but he was not with me during my hard times.

He didn't partake in some of the habits I had developed. Perry always had a clean slate. He never drank, smoked, or hung out late at night at parties. When I saw the light, that very day he said I could call him for anything and he would call me for nothing. I am honored.

<u>Timothy Rodgers</u>

It amazes me how my mother integrates back into the majority of my life. . . While she was working at the Brooklyn Hebrew Home and Hospital, as head supervisor, she met and befriended this great young guy named John Rodgers. He was my age, and she talked about him with immense admiration. I thought he was an angel in disguise from her stories and comments. Meeting him and his family marked a pivotal moment in my life. Enter his younger brother, Timmy… now my life really begins.

I could write a movie entitled, "The Adventures of the Dynamic Duo." The old adage, 'Iron Sharpens Iron'— that's the two of us. 'Slim' was much shorter and younger than I, however he referred to me as his younger brother. Because of our genuine love for each other, we both became indoctrinated into each other's families which gave us two mothers, two fathers, and gave me a much larger immediate family than my sister and I.

From Coney Island to Washington D.C., from Franklin K. Lane High School to James Madison High School, from Newburgh to New York, over to Madrid, Spain, and then the Canary Islands—we would only just be touching the surface. . . I cannot speak on the love, respect, and motivational techniques that have been utilized to empower each of us by one another. The friendly competitiveness we shared never bought any friction, only encouragement, even to the point where we both had our first homes two exits away via the Southern State Parkway in Long Island. From junior high school up to today, he has conquered the seemingly unconquerable. A great preacher, uncle, grandfather, father, husband, and my friend…

Will Bogle

Bogle, I could not thank you for the friendship we share and the love you have for my two girls. Your kindness toward EJ was Immeasurable and did not go unnoticed. You're the greatest.

Will Bogle, your presence in our lives has been nothing short of a blessing. From the very first day, your warmth and generosity have touched us in ways that words can barely express. The laughter and wisdom you shared have left a lasting imprint on our hearts. Your ability to make everyone around you feel special and valued is truly a rare gift, and it's something we'll always cherish. The world needs more people like you, whose kindness illuminates the lives of everyone they meet. Thank you for being a true friend and a source of unwavering support and love.

Your love for my daughters has been a beautiful testament to the depth of your character. Watching you interact with them, nurturing their dreams and always being there with a guiding word or a gentle smile, has been heartwarming. You've shown them what true compassion and friendship look like, and they are better people for having had you in their lives. Thank you for everything, Will—the world is indeed a brighter place because of you. We hold you dearly in our hearts and will continue to celebrate the remarkable person you are.

AFTERWORD

Since I did it. . . I know you have the ability as well.

As I summarize some of my thoughts on this journey called life, I absolutely know you have enough to live your life in abundance. This does not mean billions or even millions. . . It means the utilization of our own mind, filled with wealth, which will open doors to a brilliant array of ideas, concepts, interpretations, and answers within. In simple terms, strength and power are not the missing link. Many think in order to achieve anything one needs to be able to lift weights and carry the luggage of life. I say, "Rest, think, and grow that inner thought until it becomes reality." How many times have you seen something done or watched something be built and you say, 'I was just thinking about that' or thought 'I could have done that as well'? Just know that the same ideas you are seeing came from the same place your answers are coming from: inside!

You can live your life knowing categorically, greater things shall you do. Think outside the box… It's the box that squeezes the life out of you. Let's not equate our failures or successes to others but tune into our inner capabilities and see the "Writings on the Wall." It's invisible to others, but plain as daylight to you. . . Just look and live. My family looks inside and lives outside the box.

The metaphorical saying, 'Pick up that ax and begin to chop down that tree in your life' is a pictorial analogy meaning that massive success is the greatest testament to your victories. Always remember you are filled with wonderful working powers. It's bubbling, bubbling inside. Use that power to conquer the seemingly unconquerable things that make your road rough and your going tough. Every hill is not hard to climb. Just put one foot in front of the other and go for it.

There is no reason for you to allow seconds to slip into minutes, and minutes into hours, and hours to slip into days. Not to mention days and weeks slipping into years. Wait! Am I saying that we can look around and find ourselves in the same place three years from now? Yes. I am. I remember taking my daughters to the block that I grew up on 40 years ago. The first thing I saw were three guys sitting on milk boxes in front of the corner store playing cards. The best way to bring that to a halt is to stop now and move forward and upward. It's the bottom that is crowded. Just shake off the doubt and see how far you go after digesting this book. In the words of President Obama, 'Yes we can' and that's because 'The Answer is Within.'

As we move into 'The Answer Within' we know that it emphasizes a subtle yet direct path to problem solving and the hustle we've had with us for a long time. Sometimes we carry these unhealthy roots of failure so long until they become second nature to our real nature which is our true selves. It gives more to and encourages our resilience to propel ourselves to higher heights. I believe this book will pour an abundance of new life into you and let you know that the answer within is not relegated or delegated to a select group of people on the other side of the track. I have friends from all walks of life and you are one of them. With that, if you want anything bad enough and you just can't live without it—just 'Stop, Look and Listen' because The Answer is Within.

-Bobby Banks

I could not have done this without you.

Some people teach you what to do… Some people teach you what not to do .Wife (Gone but not forgotten) Elaina Joy Sanabria Banks Love You Until 8x8x8=4.Mommy Jessie Banks My Rock.Daddy Leroy Banks "Jessie, that boy ain't gonna **do nothin' but play the piano"** .Freida (My Mother, Aunt, Cousin and Friend) **.Sister Sharon Banks Williams PhD** My Forever Guiding Light **.Lloyd Wilams, Closer than any brother** .Brother Charles Mack . Son Leroy Banks III .Daughter Syreeta Banks **My ride or die by way of Brewster** .Son Christopher Bobby **Banks My Name Sake .Son Brian Banks Strength Personified** .Daughter Mya Banks My **Broadway Star** .Daughter Belle Banks **Rap on My Sweet One**

.Son In Law Christopher Bowen, You married my heart .LaShai Williams, PhD My Inspiration .Bijan Williams, Dance Like No One's Watching .Alix Washington, DC all the way .All my Uncles and Aunts in Heaven .All my Cousins .Dr. Donna Mendes I will forever love you, Thanks Much .Yvonne, Bridgette, and Ella, my other sisters .Sheila Sanabria, Thanks for Sharing and Being Who You Are .Uncle Charles Sanabria .Stanley Brown .The Children of God, My beginning .Corey Henry .Best Friend, Will Bogle .Debbie Williams, The funniest person I know .My confidant & Best Friend, Perry McNeil .Sidney Grayson .Bishop Eric Figuora (for life) .Rev Clarence Norman Sr. PhD .Joan Rodgers .Stephanie .Rev Chapman .Pastor Brooks & Bethel AME Church Family .Rebecca .Lorraine Bennett Wow! In the mist of my storm .My team at Madison Square Garden .Art Moore Thank you for a Golden Opportunity with ABC .Michelle Pratt Wow! I'll never forget .Trey Whitfield School .Ronald David Smith, My Mentor .Bishop Albert Jamison (for life) .Aretha Franklin, Thank You...Radio City .Rev Johnny Ray Youngblood PhD .Michelle Merchant, J.D. my friend .Best Friend, Timothy Rodgers .Patti LaBelle, Thanks for Your Hospitality .Gail Alexander Strong, biblical and Gentle .Beth McKenzy .Janie Whitney .Butch Hayward .Ron Bailey .Les Brown .JBF Team .AB Whitfield .Diana Ross .Tracey Davison Mendoza, .Miguel & Roberto I'm so proud of you

.Vince
Carless
.Ann Simmons
Brother
.Rumpus,
.Adrianna
Unwaivering
.Dan
.Marc
Blanco
in Far
my utmost
support a n d
have been instrumental
remain unnamed in this
influence and unwaiv
have profoundly
my path
I am eternally thankful.
Answer

Hudson
.Yvonne Kennedy
.Brother and Sister
and Sister
Thank You .Soda
Hackett, T h a n k
Support and
Cooper .Dr. Terry
Kauf man
.All My
Rock away
gratitude to those
pivotal contribtions
in my journey, y e t
work. Your invaluable
ering encouragement
s h a p e d
and for that,
You are "The
Within"

.Natalie
.Helen Allen
Milton Brown
Alfredo Hunte
.Ms.Glassco
Thank You
You For Your
Kindness
Grant
.Lucy
Children
.I extend
whose

PUBLISHER'S NOTE

Everyone has a story to tell, and it is befitting that this amazing story of life, with its textures, flavors and fabric, be told by one of the greatest storytellers living among us today. It is said that one can gauge God's intention for an individual by the caliber of the people placed in their path. Bobby Bank's life thus far is an essay of great relationships, competence, and experience. Much like his industry name, 'The Music Man,' the lyrical content of his life is woven within the tapestry of mankind.

There's a little bit of Bobby Banks in all of us and his celebration of people plays throughout the words of this book, in the key of love, and in the accompaniment of sharing.

This book should be required reading for every family construct and every young boy and girl as a companion of passages in an ever-changing world experiencing an identity crisis.

Sean Cort
Publisher and Friend